Edward Marshall Boehm

Portrait by Alexander Clayton · 1969

EDWARD MARSHALL BOEHM

1913 · 1969

BY · FRANK · J · COSENTINO

Library of Congress Card Number 75-130889

© 1970 by Edward Marshall Boehm, Inc.

Second Printing–1975

About The Author:

Frank Cosentino was born on April 20, 1934 in Sparkill, New York. He majored in geology at Princeton University, graduating in 1956 with a degree in Liberal Arts. From 1956 through 1958 he served in the Judge Advocate General's Corps of the United States Army, after which he joined the firm of Edward Marshall Boehm.
In 1960 Mr. Cosentino wrote his first book about Mr. Boehm. Presently he is Managing Director of Edward Marshall Boehm, Incorporated. His work includes annual lecture and exhibition tours throughout the United States.
Mr. Cosentino brings special insight into the ceramic studio because of his dual role as personal friend and business aide of Edward Boehm. He experienced the daily activity and genius of the late artist; and he continues with Mrs. Boehm and her staff in perpetuating the American hard-paste porcelain art of Edward Marshall Boehm.

Consultants:

Mrs. Edward Marshall Boehm; Harold Claassen, Editorial Staff of The New York Times; and Carl C. Dauterman, Curator, Western European Arts, The Metropolitan Museum of Art.

Design:

Mrs. Edward Marshall Boehm; Frank J. Cosentino; and J. D. Williams, Visual Motivations Foundation, Morrisville, Pa.

Frontispiece:

From a portrait by Alexander Clayton, Dallas, Texas.

Sketches:

Sketches, including the end papers of the regular edition, are reproduced from originals by Edward Marshall Boehm.

Photography:

Color and black and white photographs by Charles P. Mills, Jr., Charles P. Mills & Son, Philadelphia, Pa.

PRINTED IN THE UNITED STATES OF AMERICA
THE LAKESIDE PRESS
R. R. DONNELLEY & SONS COMPANY
CHICAGO

To President and Mrs. Dwight D. Eisenhower
with deep appreciation for their encouragement

Mrs. E. M. Boehm

Dedication . . .

To Her Majesty Queen Elizabeth II and His Royal Highness The Prince Philip October 1957 From The President and Mrs. Eisenhower

6

DDE

GETTYSBURG
PENNSYLVANIA 17325

August 25, 1967

Dear Mr. and Mrs. Boehm:

Mrs. Eisenhower and I are **deeply** complimented by your plans to dedicate your next book to us. It is gratifying to learn from a letter from Mr. Becker that Mr. Boehm's design of, "The Polo Player," which we presented to the Royal Family of Britain, helped to bring wide recognition of the excellence of his work.

His reputation as an outstanding artist is well deserved and his contributions to America's standing in porcelain art are important and enduring.

Mrs. Eisenhower and I wish a great success for the new book, as well as health and happiness to you both.

Sincerely,

Dwight Eisenhower

Mr. and Mrs. Edward M. Boehm
25 Fairfacts Street
Trenton, New Jersey

C O N T

THE SKETCHES ON THE END PAPERS AND THROUGHOU

8

ENTS

BOOK ARE TELEPHONE "DOODLES" BY MR. BOEHM

Foreword

BY BISHOP JOHN J. DOUGHERTY

It is a rare and lovely experience to visit the picturesque and enchanting aviaries of the late Edward Marshall Boehm at Washington Crossing in New Jersey. The sight and sound of exotic birds from distant lands captivate the senses and fill the heart with wonder and delight. How absorbing a lesson in the art of porcelain making to visit the atelier in Trenton and see the long and delicate process by which the birds, in a revealing moment of life, are captured in art objects of perennial beauty. The book before us will allow the reader to share in some measure these experiences. In the quiet manner of books it will evoke the sights, the sounds, the flights of the beautiful living things that inhabit the aviaries. In the gentle manner of books it will reveal the delicateness of form and color of the porcelain art.

Every book is a personal experience for the reader for good or ill. This book will be a good and civilizing experience. It enshrines a testimony to nature and to art, and God makes an eminent revelation of himself in both. It bears a gift of things to be felt and to be enjoyed, and will entice the reader to seek out the Boehm porcelains.

It is pardonable for Americans to feel a sense of pride in the notable and distinguished work of Edward Marshall Boehm, for because of him Trenton takes its place in the list of great porcelain centers like Meissen, Staffordshire and Limoges. This New Jersey artist has taken his place in the long procession of artists and craftsmen that goes back to China more than two thousand years. His masterful creations repose in places of honor in palaces and museums and homes around the world.

Edward Marshall Boehm has passed from life to death. It is given to few men to achieve immortality in time as well as in eternity. To him it is given for he has created with his mind and heart and hands immortal monuments in porcelain art that will ever bear his name. He has given his creations everything but life, and for this we are most grateful to him and to God who gave them life.

John J. Dougherty
PRESIDENT, *Seton Hall University*

Introduction . . .

BY MRS. EDWARD MARSHALL BOEHM

I have been privileged and enriched to have shared twenty-five years with Edward Marshall Boehm as his wife and partner. For twenty of those years we worked side by side establishing our studio, fulfilling our mutual goals and desires. He gave me love, a sense of destiny, and motivation in the pursuits of excellence and beauty. To recount the challenging and exciting events, from the early years through the bountiful ones, would more than fill this volume.

Perfection, drive and "win" comprised Ed's daily diet in his approach to his art and to living. The determination and intensity that possessed him affected all who worked with him. He helped each of us accomplish so much more than we might have—simply by making us believe that we could.

This is part of Ed's legacy. His staff and I, those of us whose lives he most influenced, are to carry on his work as he taught us, and as he wished—at the farm with his prized animals, the gardens and aviaries with his flowers and birds, and in the studio where he expressed his love of nature and beauty in hard-paste porcelain.

In introducing this book about my beloved husband, Edward Marshall Boehm, I take the greatest pleasure in thanking, with affection:

Our nieces, Terry and Fran, who lived with us and gave us four extremely happy years of "family" life.

My housekeeper, Haralene Hood, who cared for Mr. Boehm for eighteen years during my extended business trips, and who remains with me as my good friend and helper.

All of our craftsmen at the porcelain studio, from the youngest to the most senior, but especially our key artisans and others on our staff who worked closely with Mr. Boehm for most of the twenty years—Dominick Angelini, Helen Chesters, Raymond Coughlin, Gertrude Davis, Anthony Dragonetti, Maurice Eyeington, George Glenn, John Goodballet, Percy Hallmark, William Kazmar, Ernest Lindner, Frank Surro and Elaine Swain.

Frank Cosentino, Managing Director of our firm and author of this book as well as a prior one.

Our curators and managers at the aviaries and farm— Charles Everitt, Edwin Hart and Albert Mitchell.

The patrons and students of Mr. Boehm's art whose appreciation and interest were essential inspiration and encouragement for him and his artisans.

The fine stores and galleries, and their principals, of past and present associations.

The dignitaries, museums and publicity media which have been so important in endorsing and presenting Mr. Boehm and his art.

Meakin and Ridgway, Inc., and Minton, Inc. for handling the distribution of our art during a pleasant twelve-year association, 1956 to 1968.

Mr. Harold Claassen, of the editorial staff of the New York Times, for editing the manuscript of this book; and Mr. Carl C. Dauterman, Curator, Western European Arts, The Metropolitan Museum of Art, for his assistance with the section, "Historical Reference."

And to the many others unmentioned who, through the years, gave assistance and friendship to Mr. Boehm and to me.

I hold all very dear.

Edward Marshall Boehm, *The Ceramist*

An Appreciation by John E. Hartill

John E. Hartill,
PRESIDENT, *British Pottery
Manufacturers' Federation, 1966-1967,*
and
MANAGING DIRECTOR *of Minton China,*
Stoke-on-Trent, England.

From the history of fine porcelain, as old as civilisation itself, there emerges more clearly than from any other source that element of discontent in man from which all progress springs. In rare individuals, this becomes a passionate hunger that can be assuaged only by an extensive search for truth and beauty, by the unceasing development of talent in the creation of works of outstanding and lasting merit. Paramount was this quality in Edward Marshall Boehm.

One has to attempt to cast one's mind far into the future in order to evaluate in true perspective the work of an artist of our own generation. In ancient China, those who strove for perfection in porcelain had the blessing and support of the Emperor. In eighteenth century Europe, kings and noblemen, regardless of expense, vied with one another to set up their own porcelain factories. The historian of the future will record that Edward Boehm had no such patronage or financial backing, that with only the unswerving faith in his genius of Helen, his wife and devoted helper, who has done so much to spread his fame, he was the first in the whole American Continent to achieve recognition by heads of state and leading connoisseurs for fine hard-paste porcelain of artistic and technical excellence, not only in the United States but widely throughout the world.

Collectors in generations to come, who marvel at the perfection of his sculpture and his colouring, may well wonder

what manner of man was this, who, with no previous knowledge of the complex difficulties of hard-paste porcelain manufacture, succeeded, in an incredibly short time, where others
failed. The answer may in part be given by one of the few
who was privileged to see him at work, and to spend many
agreeable hours hearing his somewhat unorthodox philoso-
phies. Edward Boehm's original thinking, his scorn of popular
mass opinion, were at one with the endless flow of ideas that
sprang from his restless mind, ranging from mechanical de-
vices never before used in the manufacture of porcelain to
equally ingenious suggestions in overcoming any kind of difficulty that might arise. His affinity for birds and animals was
matched by an intimate understanding of their habits and
characteristics as well as of their anatomy. His deep insight

*Mr. Boehm with
a selection of
his porcelain
horses*

15

into natural history never limited his wonder for the ways of nature.

While in the opinion of those best qualified to judge, he achieved his own high standard, whether in the breeding of an animal or bird, or the creation of a Japanese garden or a porcelain masterpiece, his search for perfection was never fulfilled, and he was ever impatient to move on and conquer peaks as yet unclimbed.

Some critics, steeped in the tradition of the finest European porcelain statuettes, over-accustomed to their highly glazed finish, found difficulty, in the early days of Boehm, in approving the matt texture of his porcelain. They soon came to realize that his extensive study of all the European porcelains, from Meissen onwards, before perfecting his own techniques, led him rightly and courageously to solve a problem which faced former ceramic sculptor-designers, by firing his colours directly on to hard bisque porcelain, his formula and firing temperature providing the ideal durable and vitreous body for this purpose.

The well known sculptors who designed for the leading English manufacturers of Parian china in the early nineteenth century were well aware of the value of Parian as a medium for the reproduction of their models because the finest detail was not obscured by the gloss and thickness of a glaze covering. In the latter part of the same century, Solon reluctantly accepted the glazing tradition by exaggerating all details, both with incised lines and raised touches of "slip." In his own words "It is the only way of securing clearness and brilliancy to the details when all is bathed in a thick coating of transparent glaze."

In Boehm figures such artificial accentuation is unnecessary. The execution of the feather of Boehm's Rufous Hummingbirds, and the petals of the Icelandic poppies in the same model, finer by far than most detail in Parian figures, provide a typical example of the value of hard bisque. Parian and Solon's Pâte sur Pâte were not normally coloured, and a further advantage of the absence of gloss is the infinitely greater fidelity of the colours of nature in Boehm birds and flowers.

At one memorable gathering, when a superb collection of Boehm sculptures was presented to a cultural centre, Edward Marshall Boehm was described as the ceramic genius of the age. In more ways than one, he has made ceramic history in the twentieth century, and future generations will recognize his work as an important contribution to the art of our time.

J. Lindsay Almond, Jr.
JUDGE, *U. S. Court Of Customs and Patent Appeals*
Washington, D. C.
GOVERNOR, *Commonwealth Of Virginia*
1958–1962

Edward Marshall Boehm, *The Artist*

An Appreciation by Judge J. Lindsay Almond, Jr.

At the Boehm home, spring of 1960, Governor and Mrs. J. Lindsay Almond, Jr. with Mr. Boehm and one of his Macaws

Poor indeed is the man whose heart is not warmed, whose soul is not inspired, whose mind is not enriched by the indescribable colors with which the Creator has painted the birds and flowers of his world. To every person so moved there is always the yearning to copy the beauties of nature. Yet how very few are endowed by the Master Artist with that ability.

Each generation produces many persons who love, cherish and understand the beauties of the world but many generations may come and go before a true artist is born. That soul which can take the celestial fire and with it fashion from lifeless material an object of beauty with the expression of a vibrant and living form—a bird whose feathers invite the gentle stroke of affection, a flower ready to be plucked or a piece of fruit to be tasted.

Such an artist was Edward Marshall Boehm—a soul inspired by God, a mind and hands disciplined by innate genius to create the perfect, a heart filled with a consuming

*The Peruvian
"Cock of the Rock",
among the rarest
of Mr. Boehm's
Aviary inhabitants*

love for the beauties of nature and its living creatures. With his love and skill he created masterpieces of porcelain that defy description and enrich the lives of his fellow men.

It was a memorable day in our lives when first we saw the porcelain "Cardinals" fashioned by Edward Marshall Boehm, and an even more important day when we met the artist and his wife. They gave us a priceless gift, for from that day we were privileged to call them friends.

Not until we met Edward Marshall Boehm and saw his work did we realize the many things in nature we had longed for and all the while had missed. We began really to know and appreciate the glory and beauty around us, the flowers and especially the birds. Each little feathered creature became a warm and personal friend. And as we were able to collect and own Boehm porcelains each new piece brought a warmth of deep contentment and with it an appreciation of the genius and artistry of a master dedicated to the creation of true beauty as exemplified by God's handiwork.

Rich beyond measure is the individual who can collect and live daily with the porcelain creations of Edward Marshall Boehm. A home is made beautiful with these lifelike porcelains that will be a joy forever.

18

Historical Reference . . .

The Art of Ceramics

Mr. Boehm shown above sculpturing a large swan for placement in "Indian Gardens" (summer of 1961)

In the creation of all art forms the artist must master certain materials, elements and principles. The painter uses pigments to organize a flat, two-dimensional form and composes with elements of shape, color, light, line and texture according to principles of harmony, emphasis, proportion and rhythm.

The sculptor in the round may use wood, stone or metals and organizes in three-dimensional form through carving or building. He works in accordance with the same principles, composing with elements similar to those of the painter, but he is concerned also with volumes, planes and contours.

The architect must be aware of the tools and techniques of both the painter and the sculptor and, in addition to visual form, he must be guided by the structural soundness of his creations.

Porcelain art, to the degree developed by Edward Boehm, required the unique combination in one man of the talents of painter, sculptor and architect. To this we must add a thorough knowledge of ceramics and the subjects to which his creative efforts largely were directed.

This degree of versatility in one man is rare, and it is only through the requirements of a complex medium like porcelain, coupled with the beginnings of a small studio, that such versatility could develop. This is an important facet of Mr. Boehm's experience. The fine porcelain sculptors of history, *Kaendler, Bustelli, Doughty,* etc., all worked with established factories and concentrated primarily on the creative work, the sculptural prototypes. Supporting casts were present and skilled, qualities and formulas tested and established, reputations well known, markets oriented.

"He knew nothing about ceramics ..."

When Edward Boehm started his studio in Trenton, New Jersey, in 1950, he had only an innate talent as a sculptor and craftsman and the potential for versatility and excellence. He knew nothing about ceramics and had no formal art education. Furthermore, throughout his career as a ceramist, he refused to set foot in another ceramic factory or studio.

To understand the artist's contribution it is necessary to examine the ceramic media technically and historically. There has been a long-continuing evolution of ceramic history and knowledge, with the work and experience of countless numbers as foundation for current practices. This evolution was from East to West, beginning in the Orient well before the birth of Christ, proceeding to what is now Europe, and finally coming to the Western Hemisphere.

Within each country steeped in fine ceramics production areas grew, and studios, factories and craftsmen congregated, as industries will—*Chingtechen, Dresden, Staffordshire, Stoke-on-Trent, Trenton.* Through "peak" periods ceramic establishments in these areas proliferated (in Trenton alone, since the turn of the century, more than ninety ceramic studios were started).

Each studio had its own formula, its own secret "recipe," which it guarded carefully. The formula was memorized by the head chemist and he would divulge it only to his son or a designated co-worker. To emphasize the distinctiveness and quality of its *paste*, each studio also enjoyed giving its *ware* a special name. The result was that within a ceramic locality a jargon would develop unique to that locality. Viewed regionally, then globally, one can visualize the disparities of ceramic "language."

Further complicating the history of ceramics was the tradition of great secrecy of the early factories when, in the

seventeenth and eighteenth centuries, few of even the ruling monarchs were fortunate to have, or to be able to subsidize, a porcelain factory. When fine porcelain first was introduced to the Continent its beauty, quality and durability surpassed anything being produced in the West. The artisans and craftsmen of the Continent were not prepared to compete with the Oriental *hard-paste* porcelain. Their experience and knowledge were with pottery-type products and soft porcelains (*soft-paste*), while the Chinese had been making hard-paste since around the birth of Christ.

"...Oriental hard-paste porcelain..."

The monarchs of the fourteenth to seventeenth centuries had no choice but to vie with each other as collectors for the meager quantities of Oriental hard-paste pieces being sent west while at the same time setting their chemists and alchemists to work in hopeful attempts at duplicating the Chinese formula. When hard-paste finally was perfected on the Continent early in the eighteenth century it is no wonder that such great value was attached to the "rediscovery" and arcanism and intrigue quickly evolved.

Some of the early hard-paste factories were purposely placed in small, obscure towns, or in some other way removed from the influence and observation of neighboring factories. Pirating of skilled help and ideas became rampant and plagiarism was almost uncontrollable. Famous craftsmen like *Joseph Jacob Ringler* sold their services and "secrets" of manufacture for great sums and made an art and livelihood of arcanism. Many good factories were closed by profiteering competitors inveigling information and help, then reproducing and selling copies for less money. In some cases copyists actually improved on the originators; and there are a few cases (*Lowestoft*, e.g.) where the originators came right back and improved on the copyists! Hallmarks were duplicated expertly. Occasionally firms would even eliminate hallmarks to avoid identification.

Present students of ceramics are confronted with a long, shrouded history and a varied jargon, not to mention the inherent technical complexities of ceramics.

"...a long, shrouded history..."

*Mr. Boehm sculpturing
an original model
in plasteline*

The Media

There are three basic groups of ceramics—*earthenware, stoneware* and *porcelain*. These groups vary in types of clay used, refinement of materials, amount of vitreous content and firing temperatures.

Earthenware is a low-fired, opaque ceramic generally exposed to less than 1250° F—a "baked" body lacking the strength and hardness of stoneware and porcelain and the vitrification of the latter. The result is a porous ceramic; colors quickly are absorbed and will not sit on the surface with intensity as with stoneware and porcelain. Lack of strength and vitrification allow easy chipping and breaking and dictate that earthenware must be cast more thickly.

Stoneware basically is an earthenware formula to which *flint* has been added. To properly fuse this composition requires temperature levels approximating those of high-fired porcelain (2000 to 2400° F) resulting in a hard, durable *body*. Stoneware usually contains some natural fluxes and is exposed to enough temperature to allow slight vitrification.

Porcelain is a translucent composition made from a combination of vitrifying materials with clay and exposure of the mixture to high temperatures. Because of its translucency the selection and refinement of materials must be conducted more carefully than with earthenware and stoneware; and the vitrification process of porcelain making imposes greater technical and artistic demands.

Some of the better-known earthenwares are *delftware, redware, creamware, majolica, faience* and *terracotta*. Delftware has a white-bodied appearance arrived at by adding a *tin-glaze* coat. Decorative painting is applied against the white glaze. *Delft,* in Holland, established at the beginning of the seventeenth century, was famous for this type of ware, although similar wares were made before this in Spain and Italy in earlier centuries, and in the Orient before the birth of Christ.

"... and in the Orient before the birth of Christ."

Redware and terracotta are equally ancient. Redware is unglazed red pottery made from red clays high in iron content. Many Staffordshire potteries produced this ceramic during the seventeenth and eighteenth centuries. Later the redwares were glazed and relief motifs applied. Terracotta is similar to redware. It was reintroduced in an important way by *Wedgwood* during the second half of the eighteenth century and was considerably improved by better refinement and glazing.

Majolica and faience are, respectively, Italian and French ceramics similar to delftware, rather crude earthenwares covered over with white tin-glaze and colored with metallic oxides. The initial appeal of this type of ware prior to the seventeenth century was that it somewhat resembled the beautiful Chinese porcelains which the European factories were not yet able to make.

Creamware is a fine earthenware developed to allow fastidious buyers an alternative to the more-expensive porcelain. Calcined flints give whiteness and hardness to a cream-colored body composed of light-colored clays. A clear fluid glaze was introduced to this body during the first third of the eighteenth century, making creamware so appealing that it became the dominant earthenware for the next hundred years. Many factories in Staffordshire made creamware. Early important producers were *Wood* (c. 1750), *Whieldon* (c. 1754), *Leeds* (c. 1758), *Wedgwood* (c. 1759) and *Spode* (c. 1770).

Creamware dominated for a hundred years

Examples of fine-grained, high-fired stonewares are *basalt* and *jasperware*. Basalt, or *Egyptian Black* as it was originally

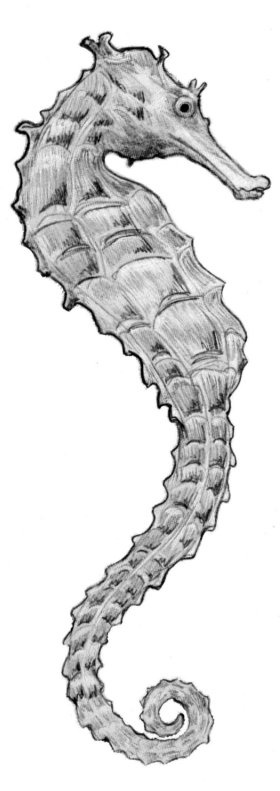

called, receives its color by the addition of manganese and iron to the composition. Wedgwood perfected basalt in 1773. Due to its ease of manufacture and its low cost and usefulness in the kitchen, it was immediately popular.

Jasper is so closely-grained it may be polished, and it is extremely durable and hard. Wedgwood introduced jasper in response to a need for a ceramic that would imitate and compliment gems—a change from the standard black and white bodies. This appears to have marked the first time that pure colors were successfully mixed with a fine ceramic body. It was probably Josiah Wedgwood's most important contribution to ceramics.

It must be remembered that, as with all basic types of ceramics, China was making stoneware centuries before the European craftsmen. The Chinese stoneware, also called *proto-porcelain*, was very similar to hard-paste because it was composed of clays rich in *feldspar*, a fusible, white vitrifying material used in making hard-paste porcelain. In their quest for the hard-paste formula, and as early as the fifteenth century, several of the early German and Dutch factories made different qualities of stoneware.

The porcelain media are fired from temperatures as low as 1250°F to a high of approximately 2400°F, depending on the vitrifying material used. Clay is the primary component serving as the nonfusible, supporting ingredient. The clay is also called *kaolin* or *china clay*. It is formed from the natural decay of feldspar from granitic-type rocks. The color of kaolin varies according to metallic content and other impurities. The whiter, purer clays are generally selected for porcelain because of their clarity, translucency of the ware when fired and better acceptance of color decoration.

Technically, the porcelain group must be divided into two categories: hard-paste (true porcelain) or soft-paste (artificial porcelain). By definition hard-paste is composed only of natural earth ingredients, primarily kaolin and feldspar. No artificial compounds are used. To properly fuse it requires exposure to temperatures at the top of the porcelain scale.

Soft-paste is composed of kaolin in combination with an artificial vitrifying material rather than the natural feldspar of hard-paste. It does not require the high firing of hard-paste.

At the top of the soft-paste temperature scale is *bone china*. Calcined animal bone serves as the vitrifying and translucent material. It proved of finer quality and strength than the earlier French and English soft-pastes where variations of glass were used. Bone has greater tolerance for kiln temperature changes, has excellent plasticity and, in addition to cutting down on kiln losses, adds a beautiful whiteness to the body.

The texture or finish of ceramics can take many forms and appearances. Fired ware with neither a glaze nor an enamel applied is called *bisque*. The bisque may be white or colored. Its most popular uses are for reproductions of statuary or to portray, naturally, subjects that do not have a shiny or glazed look. This is the finish Mr. Boehm adopted in order to depict the creatures and colors of nature with fidelity. A smooth, marble-like, matte-white soft-paste for statuary was developed in England in the 1840's. It is called *Parian*.

Glaze is a glass-like coating which renders a body impervious to liquids and helps to protect brittle ceramics from scratching or chipping. Glazes generally are made of sand and silica fused with a flux of sulphide, feldspar, lead oxide, potash or sodium chloride. If colored glazes are desired, metallic oxides are added to the mixture—tin for opaque white and pink, iron for yellows and browns, iron or uranium for oranges, copper or chrome for greens, cobalt for blue, manganese or gold for purple and maroon, iron, selenium or cadmium for reds, and a combination of iron and manganese for black.

Color may be applied directly to bisque, then glazed and refired, a process called *under-glaze* decoration. When color is applied on a fired glazed surface it is called *over-glaze* decoration.

The Evolution

Many collectors will agree that the finest examples of earthenware and porcelain are Chinese in origin. Back as early as the Stone Age they had perfected a fine-grained, hard redware. Evidence of glazing dates back a few centuries before Christ. Feldspathic stoneware, or proto-porcelain, the precursor of hard-paste, dates back almost as far. It is staggering to think that the Chinese had formulated a hard-paste during the *Han* dynasty, fifteen to seventeen centuries before the West.

Most of the early production was established near the sources of kaolin and feldspar. Chingtechen, in the vast inner province of Kiangsi, was a major center. Its location and oriental suspicion of western merchants were the major reasons the hard-paste formula was protected so well and for so long. Kilns were made of adobe-type earth and brick. After loading they were closed tightly and fired with peat and wood. The buildup of temperature was similar to that of a pressure-cooker. Measure of the maturation of each firing was inexact due to the lack of temperature control. Losses probably ran as high as 90 per cent.

Lead-glazes made green with the addition of copper were applied during the Han dynasty. Painted detail using colored lead-glaze was begun during the *T'ang* dynasty (A.D. 618-906). The most important period for the development of beautiful glazes was during the *Sung* dynasty (A.D. 960-1279) when superior vases and dishes were made and salt-glazes and lead-glazes imitated bronzes or jades.

The *Ming* (A.D. 1368-1644) and *Ch'ing* (A.D. 1662-1916) dynasties are especially important for the variety and excellence of Chinese ceramics, the initial European awareness of oriental hard-paste, and the development of a lucrative trade from East to West.

Chingtechen boomed with production. By the early seventeenth century the East India trading companies were carrying as many as 200,000 hard-paste pieces in the holds of their ships. The most popular colored glazes were of the *famille verte*, shades of iron-red, yellow, green and aubergine, and *famille rose*, dominated by opaque rose-pink.

At its peak Chingtechen grew to a heavily-populated city employing approximately a million people in the production of porcelain and involving thousands of kilns. The high level of exports was maintained to about the second decade of the eighteenth century when the Continental craftsmen finally began to learn the formula and techniques of porcelain manufacture.

From about the fourteenth century the West attempted to make hard-paste. Men devoted lifetimes to the search. All attempts arrived at varieties of earthenware or soft-paste.

The first Continental soft-paste was made in Florence, Italy, under the patronage of *Francesco de Medici* about 1580. The composition was of white clays mixed with a glassy frit and fired near the lower end of the porcelain scale. As with most of the early porcelain factories, blue under-glaze coloring was used in imitation of the popular Chinese ware. The factory was short-lived as the patron died shortly after it was begun. All porcelain progress on the Continent stopped for many decades because of the lack of technical knowledge and the difficulty of obtaining financial support.

French experiments about 1673 in *Rouen* resulted in a fine creamy soft-paste porcelain in appearance and composition much like the later English soft-pastes. The studio in Rouen was worked by a *Louis Poterat* who apparently did each piece without assistance in order to protect his secrets of manufacture. The productions of this and other Rouen studios were predominantly tablewares and vases, baroque in style and thickly potted.

Soft-paste studios also were started at *St. Cloud* (c. 1673), *Chantilly* (c. 1725) and *Mennecy* (c. 1734). These early French factories suffered because monopolies on types of paste, style of decoration and skilled craftsmen were granted to *Vincennes* in 1745 by the King. In 1753 the Vincennes factory was moved to *Sèvres* between Paris and Versailles. It was about this time that *Madame Pompadour* showed interest. With the approval of *Louis XV* she became active in the affairs of the porcelain works. Sèvres became one of the most important of all French factories. Its tablewares, in particular, are among the most beautiful ever made.

Madame Pompadour

While the French and English concentrated on the refinement and perfection of soft-pastes, German experimenters continued to work primarily with stoneware in repeated attempts to arrive at the Chinese hard-paste formula. *Augustus The Strong*, Elector of Saxony from 1694 to 1733, was a devotee of Chinese porcelain and fully supported the search for the formula. He appointed *Ehrenfried von Tschirnhausen*, a nobleman and chemist, to lead the research. Von Tschirnhausen willingly accepted the challenge as he was appalled at the huge sums of money Augustus was spending on his oriental collection, heavily taxing his people to do so.

Later (1699) an alchemist named *Johann Friedrich Böttger*, who for years had been trying to make gold for the insatiable elector, joined von Tschirnhausen. They worked for several years in the city of Dresden. In 1708 they combined an *alabaster* with kaolin, raised temperatures high, and finally made an unglazed hard-paste. In time the alabaster was replaced by the preferred vitrifying material, feldspar.

Johann Friedrich Böttger

Von Tschirnhausen died soon after the discovery. Böttger remained in Dresden for a few years and trained other craftsmen. To better protect the formula, Augustus moved the studio to *Meissen*, a small town approximately twelve miles outside of Dresden, and established the factory in a large fortress. For several decades Meissen was operated under a cloak of secrecy.

*Johann
Joachim
Kaendler*

The secret eventually spread as craftsmen left Meissen with the aid of envious and wealthy royal patrons. But none of the factories that followed was as prolific and as excellent as the great Meissen works, particularly during the period 1733 to 1775 when the creative work was under the direction of the excellent modeler, *Johann Joachim Kaendler*. The Meissen factory at its peak (which later was probably surpassed in size by some of the early English factories), produced over 35,000 pieces of porcelain in 1744.

In 1719 and 1720 ex-Meissen craftsmen helped establish hard-paste factories in *Vienna* and *Venice*. Other fine early factories were *Höchst* (c. 1746), *Fürstenberg* (c. 1747), *Nymphenburg* (c. 1753), *Frankenthal* (c. 1755) and *Ludwigsburg* (c. 1758). The *Royal Copenhagen* factory, famous for its beautiful hard-paste, under-glaze decoration, was started about 1772.

The most important of the early English porcelain factories was *Chelsea* started about 1743. The early productions were influenced by French wares and little was original in decoration or form. The founder, *Nicholas Sprimont*, was born in France, and his Chelsea paste was similar to soft-pastes of the early French factories (Saint Cloud, Chantilly, Mennecy) with which he was familiar. In time Chelsea assumed an identity of its own and fine periods of production followed in the last half of the eighteenth century. Collectors prize the many beautiful animal figures and tablewares of Chelsea.

Soft-paste English factories which modified the French-type formulas were *Bow* (c. 1748), *Derby* (c. 1751), *Longton Hall* (c. 1751), and *Lowestoft* (c. 1757). Bow made a variety of wares aimed at a mass market. Their figurines, tablewares, etc. were more topical than Chelsea's and omitted expensive decorations and similar costly extras. In 1749 one of the original Bow patent holders, *Thomas Frye*, was the first to use a quantity of bone ash in his formula—a formula that would be adopted and refined by early nineteenth century English factories.

Lowestoft, like Bow, concentrated on simple, useful wares with under-glaze and enameling. This factory made various types of tablewares and figurines but probably is best known for its charming miniatures of animals. Chinese blue and styles of painting heavily influenced early Lowestoft productions. Chinese motifs were produced in great quantities and falsely identified with oriental marks. It soon became difficult to distinguish origins even though the Chinese porcelain is better and whiter. Today, as was mentioned earlier, the Chinese are making excellent copies of old Lowestoft—almost as if in retribution!

The *Worcester* factory (c. 1751) leads a group of English factories that was influenced more by German and oriental hard-paste. The difference in its early paste was that *steatite* (soaprock—a natural, fusible rock) was used as the vitrifying agent in lieu of feldspar. The ware was called *soaprock porcelain*. This fine, durable body was ideal for tablewares and more advanced than the glass-frit soft-paste bodies of rival factories.

Worcester is the only remaining English factory started as early as the middle of the eighteenth century. Its interest in figure production began late in the eighteenth century and still continues. Of particular importance is the porcelain American bird series modeled by the late *Dorothy Doughty* and introduced by Worcester in the 1930's. Similar in concept to Mr. Boehm's art, they are faithfully reproduced birds with natural floral settings, a porcelain triumph of technical as well as artistic excellence. The body used for Miss Doughty's birds is soft-paste (bone china); that used for Mr. Boehm's birds is hard-paste.

Dorothy Doughty

Plymouth (c. 1768) and *Bristol* (c. 1770) are generally classified together, the former being moved to Bristol and so renamed in 1770. These were the first English factories to make hard-paste porcelain. Due to patent problems and technical difficulties resulting in high losses and imperfections, Bristol was closed after about a decade of production.

Most of the eighteenth century glass-frit soft-pastes were not economical. Kiln losses generally were at least 50 percent. At fusible temperatures glass is very unstable and does not hold shape well, characteristics which led the French to call their capricious soft-paste *pâte tendre*. One year after Thomas Frye's adoption of its use, English potters began to add bone to the composition. The formula gradually was tested and improved until about 1794 when *Josiah Spode* perfected the standard English bone china body—25 percent china clay, 25 percent china stone, 50 percent bone ash (approximate proportions).

Josiah Spode

In the late eighteenth century and early nineteenth centuries other well-known factories were begun—*Caughley, Minton, Coalport, Rockingham,* etc. *Royal Doulton* and the present *Royal Crown Derby* were started during the latter part of the nineteenth century.

New factories were springing up all over the world. Improved techniques, introduction of transfer printing and mechanization for mass production gradually resulted in enough volume to make porcelain available for all. Japan became a large producer of low-priced wares, and they can boast of quality wares such as their *Imari* and *Kakiemon.*

As fine craftsmen and their families immigrated to the United States studios were started in New Jersey and Ohio in areas where clays were good and fuels accessible. American factories had great difficulty gaining acceptance because of the volume of fine imports from firms with centuries of tradition and experience.

A few factories achieved recognition, *Burlington* in Vermont, *Rookwood* in Cincinnati, both involved in earthenware products. The *Lenox* factory has become well-known for its beautiful cream-colored china and many fine craftsmen and artists have passed through its doors. Today Lenox is one of the world's most important producers of fine tablewares.

Similar to the early experiences of other countries, American production of hard-paste has been limited. No doubt many studios attempted it but without success. The only firm that had a modicum of recognition for hard-paste was *Tucker,* established near Philadelphia about the middle of the nineteenth century. It had difficulties with its quality control and losses apparently were high. The firm lasted only about ten years.

Prior to Edward Marshall Boehm's venture in 1950, few, if any, American firms had ever made hard-paste porcelain sculpture that successfully compared with the fine centuries-old productions of Europe and Asia.

This pencil sketch by Mr. Boehm served as the basis for his hallmarks.

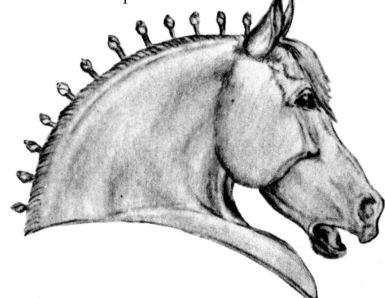

The Hard-paste Process . . .

The word *process* is ideal for introducing the techniques of making hard-paste porcelain—a seemingly endless series of fine hand-crafting steps that eventually result in a finished piece. The skills required by each step can only be acquired through years of experience because the making of fine porcelain depends as much on instinct and sensitivity as it does on instruction and learning.

Furthermore, the successful operation of a good studio (one producing fine work with public acceptance and a fair profit) requires the highest degree of coordination and sympathetic cooperation between many craftsmen of diverse talents. This is not to say that one exceptionally talented person could not in time master each of the many specialized steps. Mr. Boehm did so when he started his studio. But to multiply that excellence to some extent so that more than just a very few people could see and enjoy the art; to assure continuing quality and fidelity within the narrow confines of subject areas such as those chosen by Mr. Boehm, and to build an organization that receives sufficient economic return to perpetuate itself, requires a close, family-type team action.

This is one of the most important aspects of the Edward Marshall Boehm story. In the relatively short period of barely a decade, this total craftsman started a studio, formulated a hard-paste porcelain, learned and mastered each step in a complicated process, produced sculpture that was artistically and technically desirable, and inspired other artisans with his techniques and standards of excellence—all without formal art education or even a prior basic knowledge of ceramics.

Mr. Boehm's
La Pieta Madonna

Implementation of the porcelain process is directed by the subject matter. Therefore, it is important first to consider the motives and forces that influenced Mr. Boehm's selection of subject matter.

In the early 1950's one of the initial and strongest influences was economic. Like all artists Mr. Boehm was groping, learning the vagaries of the hard-paste medium, in an effort to create pieces which were appealing and saleable. In doing so he eventually produced over three hundred non-bird subjects, from decorative pieces to farm animals.

By 1953 he had created and marketed a few bird sculptures and it became apparent that this was his forte. Galleries and patrons gradually asked for more birds. At this point acceptance was still low and market considerations were most important. It was natural, therefore, that Mr. Boehm selected bird subjects and flowers, popular and colorful, with which the largest number of people were most familiar. This is shown by the early selections of game birds (Bob White Quail, Ring-necked Pheasants, Canada Geese, Mallards, etc.) and song birds (Cardinals, Cedar Waxwings, Blackbirds, Song Sparrows, Bluebirds, etc.).

In the second and final decade of his career, after having gained widespread recognition, the artist was free to concentrate on some of the less well-known but equally beautiful or interesting species (Green Jays, Varied Buntings, Prairie Chickens, Mearns' Quail, Common Tern, Merganser Ducks, Road Runner, Kestrels, etc.). His designs became bolder and freer. Economic considerations were relegated to a more remote position. Limitations, with the exception of artistic and technical considerations, were lifted. This movement toward freedom becomes clear when the totality of Mr. Boehm's work is viewed.

Because of the many separate steps in the Boehm hard-paste process, it is important to illustrate the scope of the total operation, then proceed to define and correlate each step. The following outlines the process:

(1) Creation of the original model in *plasteline* (modelling clay).

(2) Dissection of the plasteline model into component parts.

(3) Construction of duplicate plaster-of-paris parts by *wastemolding* the plasteline components.

(4) Refining (sculpturing) the plaster model parts.

(5) Construction of *master* (negative), *case* (positive)

and *replica* (negative) molds from the sculptured plaster model parts.

(6) Preparation and mixing the hard-paste formula to form the liquid clay termed *slip*.

(7) Pouring the slip and casting the model sections from the replica molds.

(8) Joining the cast clay sections (called *greenware*) together thereby building back to the form of the original model.

(9) Supporting and firing the greenware model into white, bisque hard-paste.

(10) Painting the porcelain.

(11) Final firings (following each painting phase) to anneal the colors with the porcelain.

(12) Final inspections.

The initial interpretation is on paper in sketch form. The bird subject is determined as are approximate size, conformation of the piece and floral complements. A rough model in plasteline then is made. Armatures are used in support of extended parts.

At this early time the artist must pause, examine the model and envision it through all stages of the process. He must be thoroughly familiar with all steps in order to sculpt a piece that is technically feasible as well as artistic. Mr. Boehm and his assistants spent weeks discussing each of the models introduced. This is the point in the process where the problems must be solved; this is the heart of the success of the porcelain venture.

Some of the important questions that must be answered are: Is the piece well-balanced? Is the size correct? Can the mold-maker perform clean, well-placed dissections? If an adjustment of form of the model is made to solve a molding problem, will it adversely affect the character and artistic interpretation? Will mold *seams* be properly located for later successful removal without harm to detail? Will the model be molded in enough components so as not to present problems for the caster? Will the cast sections which must be joined together bear precisely-fitting *keys* to guide the assembler? Has allowance been made for placement of supports to hold heavy and extended parts of the model during the initial firing? Can the colors called for by the sculpture be obtained and applied and fired accurately? After making adjustments will the final result be close to the original interpretation and goal?

Once satisfied that the sculpture is right, the chief mold-

"The initial interpretation is on paper in sketch form."

makers become involved. One might visualize the next operation on the model as that of creating a three-dimensional puzzle then proceeding to cut or jig-saw into parts that key together. The direction and number of dissections is determined by the intricacy of the model. In general the model is broken down into parts that are roughly horizontal or vertical in structure. This is to avoid the molding of complicated parts that might stick or lock in a mold. The Western Bluebirds (see page 243) required dissection into ninety-one components of base, branches, leaves and birds. To this eventually must be added forty-six azalea blooms and three-hundred and twenty-two hand-fashioned metal stems and stamens.

"...an exacting and time-consuming science..."

The making of molds is an exacting and time-consuming science. It is not uncommon to devote six to nine months to the molding of an important sculpture. Each of the plasteline model parts must have a mold built around it. The sole purpose of this first set of rough, waste molds is for casting back into them with plaster in order to make duplicate plaster model parts. This is essential because much more detail must be worked into the model and this cannot be accomplished in the soft medium of plasteline. Thus the conversion to a hard medium capable of being carved, like plaster. After refining and keying all plaster parts so they fit together, the process of mold-making continues.

Now the refined plaster parts must be molded as was done with the original plasteline parts. This time the negative impressions made in the molds bear exactly the finished detail of the refined parts. These *block* or master molds are not to be used for casting. If they were, eventual deterioration from use would force going back to the plaster model for re-molding, a procedure that is not easily repeated. Instead, the master molds are used only to make a positive set which, in turn, will be used to make another negative set exactly like the masters. The positive set is called the case. The final negatives are the replica molds in which casting of the model parts is done.

"the detail of all models remains sharp."

Normally about twenty-five castings may be taken from a set of replica molds before they begin to wear from use and saturation. The set is discarded and a new set made from the positive case. The detail of all models remains sharp. The master molds continue to be carefully preserved in the event some of the case molds are lost or damaged.

Once the replica molds are ready the slip must be prepared. The chemist first will mix and fire a small test quantity.

Ingredients from the earth vary chemically due to changing strata from which they are mined. Each new mix has to be tested and adjusted for proper whiteness, casting rate, plasticity, porosity and strength.

After testing, the kaolins, feldspar and other ingredients are poured into a ball mill that is about one-quarter filled with polished quartz pebbles approximately the size of golf balls. Liquids are added and the mill is rotated for seventy-two hours. The abrasive tumbling action of the pebbles reduces clay particles to the smallest size physically possible. This refinement procedure is critical to quality. The finer the paste, the smoother and less porous the eventual porcelain.

Over a period of time the quartz pebbles will wear into the slip as will the porcelain lining of the mills, but no harm is done as the basic ingredients are the same as those of the slip. The slip then is stored in large stainless steel tanks which have paddles that automatically stir every fifteen minutes to keep the slip from settling. When extracted from the tanks the slip is run through a de-magnetizer to remove remaining metallic impurities, and a vibrating, fine-mesh screen to separate curds or lumps.

The casters are the first sounding-boards for the work of the modelers, mold-makers and chemist. Perhaps the turn of a leaf, head or branch might be reversed to aid mold separation; a flower modeled more thickly for better support when removed from its mold; additional *props* or *bats* planned for cradling the damp clay castings. The mold-makers will learn if they left some *under-cuts* on the model that cause locks in the molds; whether the molds are comfortable to handle; and if the mold fits are sharp and tight. Finally the chemist will know the accuracy of his tests for plasticity, casting rate, etc.

". . . like a jig-saw puzzle . . ."

Each mold consists of from two to eight sections, all of which fit together like a jigsaw puzzle, yet may be drawn freely from each other without damaging the fragile clay casting inside. When assembled each mold has a pouring hole into which the caster carefully pours the slip to avoid locking of air bubbles. Several molds may be worked at one time.

When slip contacts the plaster mold, moisture begins to be drawn from it and a thin clay lining begins to build on the inside lining of the mold. In effect a positive is forming within the negative cavity of the mold. By watching the area of the pouring hole, the caster can observe the thickening cast. When the thickness appears adequate so the cast will support itself, the mold is inverted and the excess slip poured off.

In this way, all castings that have volume, the body of a bird, a heavy branch, etc., are cast hollow. Thin parts such as tongues, wings, legs and leaves are solid-cast. Hollow castings are desirable and essential; desirable because the resulting piece will be light and will show the translucency of the hard-paste; essential because it is virtually impossible to solid cast a heavy model part. As a casting thickens the rate of thickening progressively slows as it becomes more and more difficult for remaining moisture in the center of the mold to continue to pass through. In this case a wet spot would remain in the middle once the pouring hole has sealed over. In drying, the solid greenware casting normally would crack; if not, it certainly would burst when fired in the bisque kiln.

The castings are immediately placed in a damp room where moisture in the air is held at saturation. Parts must remain wet with similar moisture content in order later to be joined together.

Joining of the castings to build the greenware model is perhaps the most nerve-wracking phase of the process. Cast sections of the model are placed in a miniature damp box adjacent to the artisan. Each casting is worked with scraping tools to remove mold seams (relief lines caused by slip escaping into joints of the mold sections). Mr. Boehm and the mold-makers carefully located pouring holes so they would be incorporated in the joint areas and thus covered over as castings are keyed and stuck together. A small hole (about one-eighth inch in diameter) is bored into the underside of each hollow casting to prevent bursting when reduction takes place in the kiln.

Starting from the base and working up and out, castings are joined together by coating matching areas with a gelatinous mixture of slip, a natural adhesive. Unnatural adhesives cannot be used because of the subsequent heat and shrinkage. The castings are pressed together until they hold. Then each joint is worked with water and wooden tools called pegs until the clays actually have melded. If a joint is not melded properly, it will unknot when fired. The chances for error in clay joining increase as the number of castings increases.

The final hazard of clay work is breakage. As it dries the assembled model becomes extremely fragile, almost like pie crust. A vibration or careless move will cause the model to shatter. There is no reclamation.

Prior to placement in the kiln the greenware model must be sponged, trimmed and inspected for flaws. Then it is propped with clay crutches which support the model and hold it in balance. Props are cast of the same slip so shrinkage will be uniform. The major ones are designed when the original model is first sculptured in plasteline; others are of standard shapes and sizes and may be cut for placement under leaves and branches. Often the amount of clay used in the props will exceed that of the model.

To avoid adherence of props to models a coating of nonfusible material is placed in the contact areas. Props may be easily removed and must be discarded because shrinkage prevents their further use.

Mr. Boehm would work with his kiln-master when an original model was first propped. The kiln-master must be expert at loading, setting in the tiers of greenware and selecting a mix of different-sized models that will maximize use of available space and help equalize kiln heat.

"The kiln-master must be expert . . ."

There are two bisque kiln loading beds, each approximately three feet wide and high by five feet long. Both are stationary. When a bed is loaded the doors of the kiln swing wide and the kiln is moved over the greenware instead of the greenware into the kiln, this to avoid vibrating the fragile clay. The doors are then closed and the firing cycle begun. Heavy electrical wires in the walls, bed and doors gradually heat to 2400°F. The rise of temperature requires approximately thirteen hours.

As temperature approaches maturation the feldspar begins to melt. At full temperature it has completely engulfed the nonfusible, supporting clays. While vitrifying the model shrinks about fifteen percent, the result of alteration of the feldspar from a granular to a molten state. Approximately two days' cooling is required before the kiln doors may be opened. Although electrically controlled, the maturity also is checked by the use of pyrometric cones which are designed to melt and collapse as high temperature is reached.

On removal of the props, each fired bisque piece is inspected for defects. Those not perfect are immediately broken with a hammer. Typical defects are cracking due to faulty joining, splits due to undetected casting strains, distortion or collapsing caused by prop slippage or excess heat, and breakage through handling. Perfect pieces are sanded in preparation for the painters, and hallmark decalcomanias are placed under the bases. These hallmark transfer prints will later anneal permanently with the porcelain in the color firings.

". . . broken with a hammer . . ."

As in all critical areas of the process, mastering the techniques of applying color to hard-paste requires years of training.

The pigments are mineral oxides similar to those previously discussed as being used for coloring glazes. All are received in fine-powdered form, yet are ground further in small mills similar to the large slip ball mill. The finer the color particle size, the smoother the color when applied and fired. Our color inventory shows well over a hundred different mixtures of pigments.

Prior to application colors are mixed by each artist on a palette. Turpentine and oil are used to suspend the colors. Brushes vary considerable in size, shape and density. *Pounces* also are used, small balls of lamb's wool wrapped tightly in sheer French batiste, to draw or vignette-out a color from fulness to lighter shades.

Method of application is critical because the colors will eventually be exposed to temperatures ranging between 1280°F and 1450°F. Too much oil with the color may cause it to blister; too little may result in a spotted, uneven effect. Too light an application and the color may appear bleached from having burned away slightly; too heavy an application may cause the color to darken and possibly even flake if *piling* is severe.

Lighter colors and those which require higher temperatures for proper annealing are applied first. Then come the deeper colors followed finally by the most sensitive, lowest-fired colors, reds and oranges. Some of the models require as many as five different color-phase firings.

An important difficulty is the inability to obtain or mix certain colors. This is the reason why Mr. Boehm avoided creating such birds as the Baltimore Oriole and Scarlet Tanager. True enough colors were not available, nor could they be mixed. Also, Mr. Boehm often said that nature could juxtapose any two colors and they would seem to be in proper key and harmony; but to do the same with certain colors in hard-paste porcelain is impossible. The effect would be artificial and gaudy.

The final steps in the process are inspections of the models, the addition of finishing parts, if any (such as flowers, metal stems and stamens), and packing and shipping.

Each morning the results of the decorating kiln are carefully examined against the original, prototype model. Nothing passes that does not meet with the inspectors' approval.

These are the primary steps in the Boehm hard-paste por-

The Bird Urns on opposite page show the wide range of colors Mr. Boehm used in his creations.

celain process. Variations in individual models occur naturally
because of hand-crafting and hand-painting, movement in the
bisque kiln, and slight changes of temperature in the decorating kilns. But within these natural limitations, each model
is produced with as much fidelity and care as possible.
Mr. Boehm's artisans are dedicated to the premise that the
original model is closest to the true bird in its true surroundings.

Above: Bird Urns

Edward
Marshall
Boehm . . .

The Mar

Edward Marshall Boehm at six months in early 1914

nd The Experience . . .

● *Part I:*

A Forgotten Youth

"You can only be as good as your inheritance will allow" was a maxim of Edward Marshall Boehm, his way of explaining a person's potential. Normally a statement such as this would not seem out of character for he was often sententious and, like most deep thinkers, he combined elements of the fundamentalist, pragmatist and functionalist.

But Mr. Boehm often used this maxim in such a way that it was obvious he was applying it to himself. It appeared to be an indirect acknowledgement of those responsible for his origin and makeup, his parentage—a nod of gratitude. He did not like to talk about his early life, his family relationships or memories of his youth. Even Mrs. Boehm, in her close association with him during their twenty-five years of marriage, rarely was allowed into this part of his life.

Only once did those of us who knew him well see a chink in this armor. In the early part of 1966 a friend, Mr. George Downing, Chairman of the Board of Trustees of the Bellingrath-Morse Foundation and President of the Coca Cola Bottling Company of Mobile, Alabama, learned that Mr. Boehm's mother had been one of the famous Coca Cola Girls, symbols of health and beauty selected to represent the image of Coca Cola in the early part of the century.

Mrs. Edward D. Boehm, circa 1908

With the help of company historians, Mr. Downing succeeded in locating a photograph of Mr. Boehm's mother (see page 42) and sent it to him. Edward Boehm had really never seen his mother. She died when he was seven, a few years after her marriage failed. His image of her was vague and he had no family photos. (Those of him as a youngster on page 40 were sent to Mrs. Boehm years later by a distant relative.)

For about a day he kept the photograph to himself, savoring this important memory-tie to his early childhood, after which he carried the picture to all he knew, proudly showing his mother. For a week the photograph was not out of his sight.

"...important memory-tie..."

This represented one of Mr. Boehm's infrequent expressions of emotion. His delight was open, almost child-like. It was apparent his memories of his mother, although limited, were pleasant and warm and deep.

From that point forward, a period of approximately three years until his death, there was a noticeable change in Mr. Boehm. His manner was more relaxed, his drive for perfection and success more even-keeled, his tolerance of the frailities of those of us around him grew, and he even appeared, for the first time, to begin to understand that Edward Marshall Boehm was important to the world. Seeing his mother, which stimulated atrophied memories, and his knowledge of her great beauty, provided a new foundation, a new frame of reference for him.

Apart from this experience the few other "known" facts about his early life are as follow. Edward Marshall Boehm was born in Baltimore, Maryland, in 1913. When his mother died there were no close relatives to care for him (he was not to meet his father until he was in his twenties). Friends succeeded in enrolling him in the McDonogh School which, at the time, housed boys who had lost one or both parents.

He left McDonogh at the age of sixteen and eventually enrolled in Maryland University and studied animal husbandry. This prepared him well for farm managing. From 1934 to 1942 he managed Longacres Farms on the Eastern Shore of Maryland, specializing in Guernsey. A promising career which in 1938 had produced a Grand Champion (Norlina's Guard of Clearview) was interrupted by World War II.

While in the service he met and married Helen Franzolin in 1944 (see page 45). In this war period the farm he had managed had a disastrous fire in which most of the prized Guernsey herd was lost. He could not return to it, so he and

"...he met and married Helen Franzolin..."

Helen settled in Great Neck, Long Island, in 1945. There he secured employment as an assistant veterinarian.

The rest of the story of Edward Marshall Boehm can accurately be chronicled. It is the first three decades of his life for which biographical information is lacking.

Out of this misty background came a renaissance talent, a total craftsman and artist who would direct his being and energies toward nature, each day pursue its elusive beauty, probe its order, reach into its unfathomable depths.

A Solitary Man

Suppose one accepts that "you can only be as good as your inheritance will allow?" What of the development of that talent and its direction? What gave this person of great potential an all-consuming drive for excellence and recognition, a determination that humbled and intimidated those around him? What forces drove Edward Boehm so inevitably toward nature in daily search of origins and meanings?

"...empty and unhappy..."

The answers lie in the reluctance of Mr. Boehm to talk about his life. In his notes, letters and writings he avoided personal comments, made no references to early experiences. He wanted to blot out the early years because they were empty and unhappy. He never experienced the love and warmth of family life, the uninhibited expressions of laughter and tears between parents and child, the dependence on parental example and guidance.

His was a sterile existence. He was dependent on his own developing character and wits. Personal relationships could not influence his direction. Emotion could not interfere with his desires. In his mind, aggressiveness and determination became honed to the competition of his society. To survive in a world he found difficult to accept, he had to be equipped properly. To influence or in some way change that world, he had to set goals and let nothing deter him from them.

"...He loved God's natural world with a passion..."

His pent-up love and care found expression in God's "other world" of nature and her creatures, so much so that to see, study and understand wasn't enough. "He loved God's natural world with a passion that overflowed from him into artistic expression."

Thus Edward Boehm's avoidance of people. His most consuming relationships were with his animals. He would often say, "Animals are reliable, true in their affections, predictable in their actions." His gardens, aviaries and farm

Edward and Helen Boehm, October 29, 1944

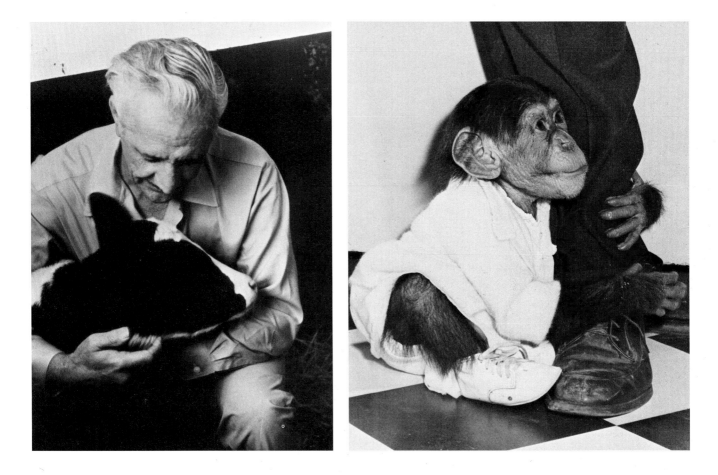

helped isolate him from society, at the same time providing inspiration and a point of reference for his art.

Yet Mr. Boehm was certainly not an introvert. The friendships he had were solid and deep and on levels ranging from prolonged, serious discussion to raucous, practical-joking fun (see page 47). In type his friends were primarily creative, scientific or involved with animals. Among them were his artisans, farmers, craftsmen of all skills, business associates, a few professional people and those involved in breeding and showing of birds, horses, cattle, dogs, fish and fancy fowl.

A Time For Fun

The older artisans at the studio are most familiar with his raucous nature. They can recall many instances when "the boss" was in the mood for fun, and once he started on you he was merciless and would quit only when your energies and his were sapped. For example, it was not uncommon to be doused by a bag of water thrown by him. I was told that in the early years of the studio, (1950 to 1955) when it was at its original location at 600 Stokes Avenue in Trenton, he actually drilled a hole in an upper wooden floor in order later to water-bomb an unsuspecting artisan below.

Above: The affinity with God's creatures

46

When a new ploy came into vogue, he was among the first to use (sometimes overuse) it. One he had a great deal of fun with was that of sending a single telegram to a distant friend which read "It is important that you ignore first telegram. Please proceed accordingly." A good many wires of this nature were sent by Edward Boehm.

Some of his schemes were grandiose. I recall vividly a time, upon his return from an African bird-collecting safari in 1959, when he arranged for a well-known animal distribution firm in New York to write a good friend that he (Mr. Boehm) had instructed the firm to deliver to the friend a baby elephant, a gift Mr. Boehm had ostensibly brought back with him from Africa!

Challenges Of The Mind

His serious discussions were as intense as the frivolous moments. He was interested in medicine and science and particularly enjoyed discussing genetics with qualified professionals. His frame of reference and "edge" were his solid and thorough knowledge of nature. He would constantly refer to the "basics of life." One of his favorite expressions was, "People just don't understand the basics." Each encounter was looked

Above shows a moment of fun in the Trenton gallery.

upon as a challenge. Later he might say, "I can always stop these guys when I want to. All I have to do is refer to practical experiences with life." or, "The old boy can hold his own. I put several questions to them that they couldn't answer."

Of his many mental challenges, the most common was word definitions or word phrases. Few days would pass that he would not come to the studio with words or interesting structures he "discovered." Most were of a scientific nature culled from various technical publications he enjoyed reading when he awakened early mornings. If you didn't know the meanings, or couldn't give close, word-derivative guesses, he would enjoy telling you of your limited exposure to things and of your need for more interests and reading.

When he was stumped on a word meaning or usage, he would go to extreme lengths. He often had us call medical, ornithological or other specialist friends long distance for assistance. The English and Science departments of nearby Princeton University became accustomed to receiving our unusual calls. He also had a penchant for coining his own word variations and phrases, and when it was pointed out that he was grammatically in error, he would rationalize in his favor by saying, "Well, it sounds right, so I'm going to use it.", or, "If it's not in the dictionary, it should be."

An Artist of Elusion

Mr. Boehm chose to remain behind the scenes in the porcelain venture as well, leaving administration of the enterprise and public appearances to Mrs. Boehm. He especially did not enjoy talking about his work or being praised for it. It embarrassed him and he felt it was unnecessary. To him his art simply was an extension of his interests and he always wondered why people made such a fuss about it.

*His art—
an extension
of his
interests*

Furthermore, he would not be part of a cocktail hour or party. He never drank; but more important, he couldn't endure the meaningless chatter and small talk, the lack of attention and concentration given to party conversation. He once said, "I think I'm sparing the other guests also. I would probably insult some of them if I went in there."

Mrs. Boehm and I often tried to convince him that he should attend certain high-level functions honoring him and his art. In most cases he refused in spite of our strong arguments and cajoling. Occasionally we would succeed, but the aftermath of each never was worth the benefits derived. Ten-

sion would build in him until he would cramp due to a condition of abdominal hypersensitivity. In turn we would wind up receiving a severe scolding in indelicate terms and with the admonishment, "Don't ever dare put me in that position again."

A few cases must be related. In October, 1958, a glamorous dinner-party at the ambassadorial level was given in Mr. Boehm's honor in Washington, D. C. About fifty dignitaries were to be present for the occasion. Mrs. Boehm went in advance to assist the hostess in her planning. As might have been predicted, Mr. Boehm never appeared. His secretary said later he got as far as the train station, was about to board, then changed his mind and went home. He simply couldn't go. The reason given in a later apology was that his allergy flared and his face swelled severely. This became a handy excuse soon to be adopted by Mrs. Boehm in her often-experienced, on-the-spot apologies for his absences.

In January of 1967 Mr. and Mrs. Boehm were honored by an invitation from the First Lady, Mrs. Lyndon B. Johnson, to visit with her at the White House. This was one invitation Mr. Boehm could not escape. The occasion was the presentation of a pair of Wood Thrushes to Mrs. Johnson for her work with The National Cancer Society (see page 49). I was privileged to accompany Mr. and Mrs. Boehm. Tea was served and the gathering lasted for about fifteen minutes. During the entire visit Mr. Boehm continually murmured to Mrs. Boehm and me, "Let's get out of here, my filly is in the seventh race at Liberty Bell and I want to see her race." He was not being disrespectful. He was uncomfortable out of his environment, and the filly was one of his prized animals. We did make it to Liberty Bell in time, and his filly won.

"...out of his environment."

Our travel agency was continually frustrated. Of all the trips planned by Mr. Boehm for which tickets were issued, probably nine of ten were canceled at the eleventh hour. At times he actually started on trips, but usually was late for his train or plane. His comment would be, "Well, I really didn't want to go anyway."

Among the techniques he had for avoiding visitors or excusing himself from people while at work were two of which I was particularly fond. At work he dressed in grey fatigue-type clothes and was usually right in the midst of the activity, so he was often taken as one of the staff at the farm, aviaries or studio. People who didn't recognize him would walk up and ask where they might find Mr. Boehm. He would say something like, "I don't think he's around today; I believe he's away for the day," and continue with his work.

At the studio, if someone came into the gallery to meet him, he would leave through the back door to avoid the encounter. On occasion he was obliged to say "hello" to important visitors. If he wanted to make it quick, before making an appearance he would go back to the mold shop, dip his arms into plaster up to his elbows, then come in and say, "Hi, just wanted to say a quick hello. You'll excuse me, I'm right in the middle of something."

The few times each year that he would leave home voluntarily were to attend animal shows or sporting events. He would visit the horse shows in Harrisburg, New York and Lexington. Two of his proudest moments occurred in the fall of 1966, when his great Holstein, "King's Arctic Rose" (see page 51), was Supreme Grand Champion over all dairy breeds at the National Dairy Congress in Waterloo, Iowa, and Grand Champion of the Holstein Breed at the Chicago International Livestock Exposition.

"Two of his proudest moments..."

His friends knew the great attraction animal competitions or sales held for him. Mr. Oliver H. Delchamps, his good friend from Mobile, used to say to me, "I can get Ed down here once in a while. All I do is wait for an important sale or show to come along and time my invitation with it."

"King's Arctic Rose" with her 1969 heifer, "Boehm's Dream." In 1966 Rose was named Supreme Grand Champion at the Dairy Cattle Congress, Waterloo, Iowa and Grand Champion of Holsteins of the International Livestock Exposition, Chicago. Rose also was All American Award Cow in 1966, a member of All American Produce that same year and, at the age of seven years, eight months was classified best producing classified cow of the Holstein breed. For 365 days, three times a day milking, she produced 35,276 pounds of milk and 1,319 pounds of fat. At this writing she still holds the world record.

Fifteen year old "Canary Pri MCC Heilo" dam of "King's Arctic Rose," shown with her 1969 heifer, "Duncravin Pattern Maker"

A Competitive Spirit

His competitive spirit and the pleasure he gained from winning or excelling naturally drew Mr. Boehm to sports at an early age. He was well equipped for it, particularly football and boxing, two sports he engaged in semi-professionally. Physically, he stood an even six feet and weighed about two-hundred pounds. This did not represent extra weight, as he prided himself on his conditioning. He was thick-framed and heavy-boned with wide shoulders and large, strong arms and hands. His skin was tough and weathered and his jaw-set was tight and broad. He moved well, with quickness and coordination.

His relaxing moments at home were spent with his television set following sporting activities on weekends and week nights. Because of my common interest in athletics, rarely an evening would go by without Mr. Boehm calling to discuss an umpire's decision, a manager's move, an outstanding performance. I was forced, more or less, to watch the same channels. If I were not tuned in to an important event, he would chide me with, "What's the matter, are you losing interest in sports?" or, "Boy, you're missing one of the best games of the year." There were evenings when he might call half a dozen times. He became so engrossed in the competition, football particularly, that he had to talk about it, to vent his feelings. When his team lost, it would ruin his day, or even trigger his stomach cramps.

Those who coached him when he was young must have had their hands full because he was not a reasonable participant. In later years he tried his hand with our company bowling team and even attempted a few rounds of golf. He was much too intense for competition. After releasing a bowling ball, he would fall to his knees, sometimes go into a prone position, pounding the floor, shouting, trying to influence the rolling ball.

Golf was quite an experience. He went on a nine-hole playing lesson with the club professional. Never again! He threw several clubs, fumed all the way, and was upset because he couldn't strike the ball as well as the pro. In addition, analyst and pedagogue that he was, he immediately started coaching all around him in the fine points of the game.

Work Not By Time

Most men of great accomplishment have similar traits, two of which are a sense of timelessness and the ability to concentrate totally on a goal or pursuit, shutting themselves off from others and from daily routine. These traits began to show in Edward Boehm soon after he and Mrs. Boehm settled in Great Neck in 1945.

The veterinarian for whom Mr. Boehm worked, Dr. Michael Berliner, fortunately was an understanding employer. With his aggressiveness and high-powered approach to things, Edward Boehm immediately tried to revamp the doctor's veterinary business. It became obvious to Helen Boehm that her husband had a unique facility for understanding animals, a sense of communication with them that was extraordinary. Although not a doctor, he seemed to know instinctively an animal's ailment and the treatment called for. He and his employer often disagreed and heated arguments would ensue. To the doctor's chagrin, Edward Boehm often was right. Perhaps this was why he continued to retain him in his employ despite their constant differences.

A second source of irritation to his employer was Edward Boehm's refusal to stick to a set work day. He would not be held to routine, to pre-set hours. He felt a person should work hard when hard work was called for. Why sit around on days when there was little to do? In the end he would put in more time and concentrated effort than the average employee. When a job had to be done, time became unimportant to Edward Boehm. Sticking with the task and getting it done right was most important to him.

Mrs. Boehm soon had to become accustomed to her husband coming home at odd hours. Sometimes he would sit with animals through the night in an effort to help them, a practice that continued through his lifetime. Mrs. Boehm can

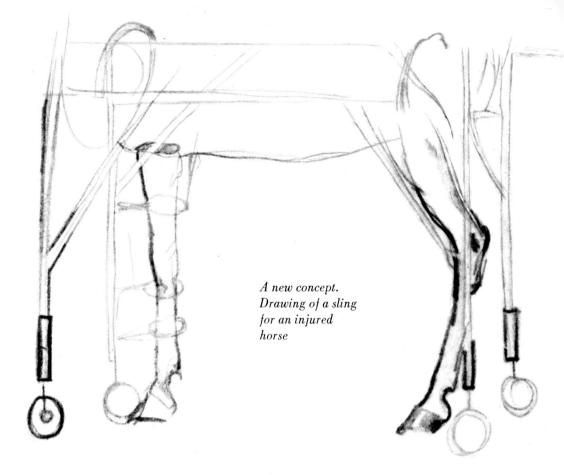

*A new concept.
Drawing of a sling
for an injured
horse*

recall the many times in later years that he would be up all night in the barn with a mare to foal or a cow to calve. He would not sleep the night an animal of his was to be born, and he never completely entrusted a birth to others.

His habit of working in spurts carried over to the studio. To work with Mr. Boehm you had to be prepared for unusual hours and conditions. He might arrive on a Friday afternoon, become interested in a specific sculpture or problem, and proceed to work through the weekend with little rest and no forewarning. He would not even want to stop for lunch or dinner. Only after long protesting by his staff would he consent to pause a few moments for nourishment. His key artisans learned to accommodate him. There was no choice.

Considering the amount of time he gave to the porcelain venture, his output was prodigious. Only about a third of his working hours was given to the studio. The remainder was divided between his farm, gardens and aviaries. There were periods when we might not see him for a week or two, particularly in the spring when the gardens were most beautiful, or when the local harness tracks were active and his horses racing.

A Sense Of Value

Helen Boehm must have been a mystified newlywed. She was raised austerely in a large family with several older brothers.

Prior to her marriage she had practically no freedom, was primarily exposed only to the mores of a close-knit family of Italian tradition. Her infrequent excursions out of her world were for educational purposes. Following high school she trained as an ophthalmic dispenser.

Edward Boehm was quite the opposite and she admits this was part of the initial attraction. He was older, represented a freedom and independence she had not experienced, and was convincing in his courtship—not to mention his striking good looks. She accommodated his whims and desires, realizing she could not constrain him anyway, and not really wanting to. But her patience and understanding were to be tested again and again, and to Helen he remained unpredictable through the years. Unpredictable but never boring.

She vividly remembers a pact they made never to tie strings, never to inhibit freedom of action. He could not live

Mr. Boehm was fascinated with the Lion Fish. He spent many enjoyable hours studying it, contemplating its feasibility as a subject for porcelain sculpture.

any other way and wanted her to have the same privilege. He exercised this privilege constantly and in unusual ways.

After a short time Mrs. Boehm realized her husband's position with the veterinarian could not be permanent. In fact, she was beginning to doubt that Edward Boehm ever could work long for any employer. She offered many times to go back to Maryland with him or to any state where he again might work with animals. But he seemed to be biding his time, getting new bearings. Another reason for the offers was that she wanted to get him back on a farm before he brought a farm menagerie to her and her apartment.

Mr. Boehm brought home dogs, fancy fowl and fish. Rarely did he ever turn over a pay check to his young wife. He much preferred to spend it on a beautiful animal. At times he would come home and tell Helen Boehm of a beautiful tropical fish he wanted to purchase and add to his growing collection. He thought nothing of paying twenty to forty dollars at a time when he could ill afford it. The money wasn't important to him, the fish was, and no reasonable price was high. He would often convert the week's grocery money into an animal. His fowl collection grew so large Mrs. Boehm

White Leghorn

Brahmin

suddenly found herself in the egg business. His kennel in the back yard also expanded and it was no wonder the couple was often threatened with ejection.

Evening activities were frequently limited to combing and washing the fancy fowl, grooming and trimming the dogs, or just sitting discussing the beauties of his creatures. He dreamed aloud of a future day when he would have his own farm, his own animals to show and breed, possibly even an aviary with beautiful birds.

Expectations

Apart from her love for Edward Boehm, what made all of this palatable for Helen Boehm was his intense love of nature and the sacrifices he would make for it. He spent little money on his person or for material things. Throughout his married life he never bought a suit, shoes or other apparel. Mrs. Boehm had to buy all of his clothing and other personal effects for him. His feelings were so deep and true they were inviolable, not to be questioned, not to be interrupted.

In his efforts to describe his feelings to her he continually sketched animals and modeled them in clay with a skill and

Black Cochin

White Cochin

FLOWERS

FIGHTING COCKS
...by Mr. Boehm at
age thirty-four

quickness that suggested many years of art training. But he had none. The excellence of his models was the result of a life-long interest in art, an innate artistic talent and the many long hours through his life spent in study and wondrous contemplation of the "other world." (The pages here illustrate three paintings, two of which Edward Marshall Boehm did between the ages of nine and eleven while at McDonogh.)

Helen Boehm sentimentally recalls their first meeting in the summer of 1944 at the Air Force convalescent center in Pawling, New York. She and her mother often visited a convalescing brother there. To while away the time the young Miss Franzolin would go to the hobby and recreation center. When she first saw Edward Boehm he was busily modeling a beautiful mare and foal. Assuming he was the art instructor,

HUNTING SCENE above and FLOWERS on opposite page were painted between the ages of nine and eleven.

she introduced herself only to find that he was not the instructor and modeled only as a hobby. He was, in fact, in charge of the cattle and canine activities of the center. In the short courtship that followed Helen Franzolin realized she loved the man and was prepared to love his interests, foreign as they were to a city girl. They were married two months after they met.

"... modeled only as a hobby."

By 1947 the small extra room in the apartment in Great Neck was filling with clay models of wild life, horses, cattle and dogs. When possible Edward Boehm would go to nearby farms on weekends and work from life. He also worked at night with Helen Boehm as his assistant. Her most trying moments would be when he would insist that she hold in a show stance for a couple of hours an unfriendly German Shepherd or Doberman Pinscher.

Like most young wives, Helen Boehm was convinced her husband had a superior talent. Fortifying her opinion were comments of close friends, a few who were discerning, that Edward Boehm had an amazing gift for sculpture. The weight of opinion gradually forced him to consider his art as a possible vocation. He came to like the idea. What better way to call attention to real beauty and conformation?

Many hours were spent discussing the different possible media for converting the sculpture. The only ones that would be considered by Edward Boehm were those that best portrayed color as well as form. This narrowed the field to ceramics. Weekends were now often spent at museums, studying collections of other artists and studios, and reading about them at home on week nights.

Hard-paste, The Royal Medium

"... no American had ever excelled in hard-paste sculpture ..."

The medium which most fascinated Mr. Boehm was hard-paste porcelain because of its beauty, its historical importance and the great challenge it offered. He was aware that no American had ever excelled in hard-paste sculpture. He saw no reason why he couldn't formulate it if the Chinese had done so as long ago as the Han dynasty. Furthermore, Trenton, New Jersey, was a short train ride away and there was a wealth of knowledge and craftsmanship in this, the ceramics capital of our country.

Through 1948 Mr. Boehm made frequent trips to Trenton and established friendships with several chemists. He came to learn that formulating a fine hard-paste was difficult but

60

not impossible. Enough material had been published about it so that the necessary types of clays and proportions of each could be ascertained. The prime reason why few attempted hard-paste was because of the extreme temperature necessary to mature it and the attendant severe problems of design, proportion and kiln support. An engineering acumen was as essential as artistic excellence in order to minimize losses while producing art pieces that were desirable. A second reason for avoiding hard-paste was because of the excellent examples imported from the fine centuries-old firms of Europe and Asia, a competition which was considered impossible to survive.

Learning this only served to spur on the determined artist. His trips became more frequent and he finally left his veterinarian position to devote his full attentions to hard-paste. Mrs. Boehm continued a position she had obtained with E. B. Meyrowitz of New York, one of the world's important optical firms, and earned enough to provide for living expenses.

By mid-1949 Edward Boehm formulated the beautiful quality of hard-paste he was seeking. He now had the formula and many models. The remaining, important problem was money with which to begin. He approached Doctor Berliner, his former employer, and the Doctor agreed to be a financial partner to the artist. They formed a company. It was called "Champions On Parade."

"He now had the formula and many models."

The Man and The Experience

● Part II:
The First Decade—
Hope And Promise

With the limited funds available, Edward Boehm rented a basement studio on Stokes Avenue in Trenton and almost daily made the trip to New Jersey and back to Great Neck. Fortunately the process of making hard-paste required very little equipment—a grinding mill, electrical kiln, and small quantities of clay, plaster and other inexpensive materials. Mr. Boehm purchased used equipment which held the initial investment down to just under a thousand dollars. By late 1949 he began transferring his first sculptures of Herefords, Percherons and dogs into hard-paste porcelain.

Anxious to be closer to his studio and to devote his maximum time and energies to his creations, Mr. Boehm decided that a move to Trenton was necessary. Because of this and the rapidly growing financial demands of the new venture, Doctor Berliner felt he no longer could assist the artist. He withdrew from the company. Edward Boehm faced a major obstacle. Without a financial partner the studio could not continue, and a move to Trenton certainly would be impossible.

He had no one to turn to but Helen Boehm. In her work with the optical firm she served a distinguished clientele. Perhaps among them might be a businessman who would invest in the studio.

Amazingly enough, she did succeed in interesting one of her clients and friends, Mr. Earl Weisbrod, and a new partnership was consummated. It was named the "Osso China Company." Edward and Helen Boehm moved to Trenton early in 1950. Now she was forced to commute daily between Trenton and New York.

The next six years were to provide moments of excitement and depression for the Boehms. In retrospect, the hand of God surely was over them for there were too many critical times in this period when it appeared the porcelain venture would fail. The great determination and endurance of Edward Boehm, working seventy to eighty hours a week, coupled with the courage, faith and enthusiasm of Helen Boehm, somehow carried them through each crisis.

"... the hand of God."

In the first full year of operation Mrs. Boehm helped in her spare time and lunch hours presenting her husband's work to art galleries and fine stores in New York. The firm certainly could not afford a sales and promotional staff so this important work fell to her. In time she realized that to perform her new responsibilities well, she had to devote full time to them. Late in 1950, with the concurrence of Mr. Boehm's partner, she resigned her ophthalmic dispensing position and joined the strained payroll of Osso.

This proved to be germinal to success for now were joined two potentially great talents. Helen Boehm was to become her husband's great devotee and booster. Through imaginative promotional techniques, a sense of propriety in business and promotional matters, and an unfailing instinct for timing she would be the person most responsible for bringing Edward Marshall Boehm and his art to the attention of the world. As Mr. Boehm readily stated, "Without her the porcelain venture would have joined the list of thousands of failures recorded in the last few centuries."

From the outset there was no question about the excellence and fine quality of Mr. Boehm's work. As early as the first week of January 1951, when Mrs. Boehm arranged for Mr. Vincent Andrus, Curator of the American Wing of the Metropolitan Museum of Art, to see the porcelains, endorsements came quickly. Mr. Andrus' statement that they were "equal to the finest of superior English work," and his purchase of two pieces for the Museum, "Percheron Stallion" and "Hereford Bull" (see pages 64, 65), brought immediate press interest.

In a January 20, 1951 article in The New York Times, Sanka Knox, art reporter, wrote in her lead paragraph, "The work of an artist newly started on a career of producing animal porcelain figures, close-to-nature models that have met the highest criteria set by dog fanciers, cattlemen and packers, recently passed the equally rigid standards of the Metropolitan Museum of Art."

"... the Metropolitan Museum of Art."

In a January 22, 1951 article the Trenton Times stated, "The prime moving force behind Osso is a graying, muscular man named Edward Marshall Boehm. He is the sculptor who designs the models and supervises them down to the final glazing. They are obviously the work of an artist who knows his animal anatomy."

Fortified with these endorsements Helen Boehm had better success in placing sculptures in fine stores. Among the first to show interest were Black, Starr and Gorham, Bergdorf Goodman and Bonwit Teller in New York, C. D. Peacock and Marshall Field and Company in Chicago, Closson's in Cincinnati, Haugh and Keenan in Pittsburgh, and Bailey, Banks and Biddle in Philadelphia.

Through 1950 the collection was modest. Mr. Boehm was still in a trial-and-error period and problems with the hard-paste formula required time to solve. Hundreds of firing tests were made utilizing simple commercial molds for the castings. (Some of these have been found by collectors in recent years.

Percheron Stallion

Hereford Bull

Their interest lies in their usually primitive appearance and historical importance. They are Mr. Boehm's paste but not his sculpture.)

Some of the first "Boehm" pieces to be introduced were Canvasback Ducks, single Wood Thrush with Crab Apple, Green-winged Teal, Wood Ducks, Leghorns, Tulip Bowl, Grape Box with Cupids, Fruit Bowl Set, Mythological Figures, Percheron Stallion, Belgian Stallion, Percheron Mare, Hunter, Red Fox, La Pieta Madonna, St. Maria Goretti, Boxer, Scottish Terrier, American Cocker, Holstein, Hereford Bull, Angus Bull, and a set of Service Plates with Demi-Tasse Cups.

By early 1951 Mrs. Boehm was able to obtain consent from a few stores to hold exhibitions of the porcelains. The first of these was in March of that year with Black, Starr and Gorham. The show was called "Champions on Parade" and coincided with the New York Westminster Kennel Club Show at Madison Square Garden (see page 61).

Mr. Boehm sculptured new models at a furious pace. Those that would sell continued to be made. Those that did not were not made again. There was no point to reproducing models that could not be sold. This is why the approximate numbers of early sculptures vary from but one to many. Pieces sat on shelves in an unpainted, bisque or glazed white state. Often these were sold as they were or were given away to staff and friends. Thus early subjects exist in three finishes—glazed decorated, glazed white and bisque white— although the number of early bisque pieces would be few.

Pointer and Red Fox

Edward Marshall Boehm, Inc.

Sales were slow, much too slow for financial partners. Mr. Weisbrod withdrew in early 1953. Again Mrs. Boehm was fortunate to locate an interested investor, Mr. Tom Jordan of New Orleans, who also was to remain a friend of the Boehms after their later disassociation. Mr. Jordan is a connoisseur of fine porcelains and was fascinated by the fine hard-paste pieces of Mr. Boehm. Because of the individual recognition the artist had received from the Metropolitan Museum of Art and the press, it was decided the firm should be renamed Edward Marshall Boehm, Incorporated.

But this partnership too, quickly was dissolved due to continued heavy financial losses. Yet the Boehms were not disheartened. Feeling that they were on the brink of success, that three years of hard work and heartache soon would be rewarded, the determined couple held on.

Almost immediately their fortunes seemed to change. Now working for themselves alone their spirits lifted, their energies were renewed, their optimism revitalized. Edward Boehm continued to turn out fine porcelains while Helen Boehm, now traveling as much as ten months a year, scheduled exhibition after exhibition, bothered the press for attention everywhere she went (and got it), and left in her wake a

Mischief and Innocence

ULPTURES...

growing list of retail admirers who marvelled at her enthusiasm and dedication.

The effect of Mrs. Boehm's influence is expressed in a January 19, 1953 New York Herald Tribune article which stated in part, "Dark-haired and vivacious Helen Boehm is tremendously interested in her husband's work which she believes is making a substantial contribution to American art heritage. To hear her talk about him makes one a believer."

Retail executives who had art buying positions in fine stores still remember Helen Boehm's first calls. Recently Mr. Hubert St. Onge, formerly with a store in Boston, later with Minton, Inc., of New York, told me of the time Mrs. Boehm first called on him in the early 1950's. He recalls going home that evening and telling his wife that he had met one of the finest female representatives ever, that he was amazed by her enthusiasm and dynamism.

Presidential Endorsement

While calling on all promotional and publicity media in each city she visited, Helen Boehm also sought out well-known collectors and visited museums to speak with directors. Through an introduction she was fortunate to meet the late

Jesse Jones, former R. F. C. Chairman and U. S. Secretary of Commerce. Mr. Jones was intensely interested in porcelains and in the welfare of anything fine that was American. He purchased six of the sculptures and presented them in February, 1953 to the Houston Museum of Fine Arts: Hereford Bull, Wood Ducks, Percheron Stallion, Green-winged Teal, Leghorns, and Mallards.

That same year the Louisiana State Museum acquired three pieces: Fox Hound, Angus Bull and Leghorns. Through the 1950's other important institutions added Boehm pieces to their collections including, chronologically, The White House, Brooks Memorial Art Gallery, Los Angeles County Museum, Royal Ontario Museum, Elysée Palace, Buckingham Palace, New Jersey State Museum and Smithsonian Institution.

Introduction of the porcelains early in the decade to our late former President Dwight D. Eisenhower and Mrs. Eisenhower was an important and honored event for Mr. Boehm. The President and First Lady were favorites of Mr. and Mrs. Boehm and in a later year (April of 1965), at a dispersal of General Eisenhower's herd in Culpepper, Virginia, Mr. Boehm met the General and purchased one of his prized two-year-old Black Angus cows, "Black Jestress," which later had three offspring, one of which Mr. Boehm named "Duncravin Mamie."

The Eisenhowers' initial awareness of Mr. Boehm and his art occurred in February of 1954 when Mrs. Boehm wrote Mrs. Eisenhower and suggested that she present to her and The President a porcelain by American's premier hard-paste sculptor. The subject selected was the Hereford Bull (see page 65). Mrs. Eisenhower graciously accepted and invited Mrs. Boehm to the White House for lunch. A week later a letter arrived from Mrs. Eisenhower.

The friendship that developed was to carry on through the years. Presidential commissions which followed constituted the most important endorsement given in these crucial early years of the studio. It is natural and fitting that this book is dedicated to the Eisenhowers.

A Burst Of Creativeness

The character of the collection stayed pretty much the same during the first three years of the studio. New sculptures were continually added but the emphasis remained on

March 10, 1954

Dear Mrs. Boehm,

I cannot tell you how very pleased I am with the handsome porcelain bull which you presented to me the other afternoon on your visit to the White House. This gift, I know, will be one of my most prized possessions, and I am most grateful to you and your husband for your generous thought. I liked, too, the attractive way in which your package was wrapped, with the cunning little elephant on top!

It was delightful to meet you, and I was much interested in learning of your and your husband's work.

With warmest thanks and very best wishes to you and Mr. Boehm,

Mamie Doud Eisenhower

animals, dogs and decorative pieces. Our earliest existing price list, dated June 1, 1952, reveals that the birds had progressed only to the Mallards (Hallmark 406) and all subjects continued to be glazed. Old advertisements in our files show that bisque decorated birds began to be introduced in 1953. The first to be done in this natural finish were probably the Canada Geese. (It should be explained here that because Mrs. Boehm traveled constantly the first six years of the venture, complete records of production, shipping, price lists, etc., were not maintained satisfactorily.)

From 1953 to the end of 1955 introductions of new bird models accelerated. Mr. Boehm continued to create game birds, primarily: Bob White Quail, Canada Geese, Ring-

necked Pheasants, Woodcock and Golden Pheasant. The first important song birds were the Cardinals (Hallmark 415—see just above) followed by the Cedar Waxwings and Golden-crowned Kinglets. With the Cardinals and Waxwings, design became freer, the bisque decorated finish for birds was adopted totally, and for the first time Mr. Boehm gave importance in the compositions to the foliage complements. The Kinglets (Hallmark 419—see page 72) is the first subject in which flowers appear. The artist perfected a fine variation of his hard-paste formula which allowed for creation of life-thin, life-textured flower petals.

The years 1954 and 1955 were encouraging. The song birds brought new attention from collectors and sales were increasing. Financial obligations remained heavy, but the

Cedar Waxwings

burden was easing. The studio was moved to its present, larger quarters at 25 Fairfacts Street in Trenton. The staff was increased to about twenty. A promising future now seemed possible.

Mrs. Boehm was being pressed by galleries and stores for more bird sculptures and for limited edition series. She conveyed the market reactions to Edward Boehm. It became

Golden-crowned Kinglets

apparent that this was the subject area in which he should concentrate his creative energies. And concentrate he did. The next thirteen-month period, January 1956 to February 1957, proved to be one of the most prolific of his career. In this span were completed original models of Song Sparrows, Blacktailed Bantams, Carolina Wrens, Cerulean Warblers, Red-winged Blackbirds, Downy Woodpeckers and American Eagle, plus a few smaller bird subjects. The years of hard

Song Sparrows

work, study, and trial and error culminated in this burst of creativity.

The Song Sparrows (directly above), which were to become one of Mr. Boehm's most important compositions, gave evidence of what was to come in future years. The pulpy-look of the graceful leaves and stems, flowers that seemed to be frozen from life, the ornithological perfection and grace of the birds, and the charming back-yard setting of the flower pot and trowel captivated all who saw the sculpture.

But the market still was not well-oriented to Boehm. The Song Sparrows and companion subjects were too ambitious, too many and too soon. Acceptance of them was slow and orders from galleries and stores were meager. But Edward and Helen Boehm both knew that it would be only a matter of a little more time before collectors "discovered" them. Undaunted, Edward Boehm did not let up his pace through 1957 and 1958, but he did change drastically the character of his introductions.

In this period the fledglings were first introduced and new collections comprised mainly these small birds and other "nonlimited" models, those below limited editions in price and without predetermined numbers of replicas to be made. Of fifteen new bird sculptures, four were moderately-priced limited editions: California Quail, Meadowlark, Mourning Doves and Nonpareil Buntings.

The Twins

Edward and Helen Boehm had no children. The subject appears rarely to have been discussed. It seemed to be understood between them that their contributions were to be in other areas—in their work and dedication to excellence. One sensed their feelings that it would not have been fair to attempt to raise children between 1945 and 1955 in an environment of instability and long periods of separation. They apparently realized that to make a success of their venture required both their complete energies and time, that Mr. Boehm could not approach his elusive goals without Helen Boehm.

This is not to say they did not want children. They both loved to be with youngsters and devoted more than average attention to children of friends and to the many underprivileged.

Mr. Boehm, as has been previously discussed, was impatient with and aloof from adults and was neither complimentary nor solicitous. With children, as with young animals, he was just the opposite, and in many ways he treated all young life alike. He enjoyed teaching, disciplining and watching conformation and intelligence develop. He wasn't good at expressing affection but he obviously relished receiving it from the young.

Mrs. Boehm is overly-solicitous and overly-affectionate, as

"They both loved to be with youngsters and devoted more than average attention to children . . ."

parents of her young friends will attest. She is the only person I know for whom my daughter gladly would leave home!

In late 1955 an important and cherished experience began for Mr. and Mrs. Boehm. Their fortunes had improved and Mrs. Boehm yearned for renewed ties with her family. Her sister and brother-in-law, Mr. and Mrs. Leo D'Antona, were raising identical twins, Teresa and Francene, two lovely, dark-haired girls of high school age. With the consent of the parents, the Boehms invited the girls to live with them and attend a private school near Trenton.

For four years "Terry" and "Fran" lived with their aunt and uncle. It was a rewarding experience for all, although at the time the girls might not have agreed. Mrs. Boehm still was traveling often, so they spent much more time with Mr. Boehm. No Italian father could have been more strict! From the first day he let them know where the authority lay. He set guidelines for them and, with the help of the household maid, Haralene Hood (who still lives with Mrs. Boehm), ran the "family" with the same kind of discipline he undoubtedly received while at McDonogh.

The girls had daily chores assigned. The most difficult was caring for his kennel of approximately thirty schnauzers. Each morning before school they would rise early and feed and water the dogs. After school they would clean the pens. If a dog show were approaching, the entrants had to be bathed, groomed and trimmed.

The relationship was one of moments of fun, as well, and a time for much learning. While Mrs. Boehm was away, Mr. Boehm would take the girls to animal shows of all kinds, farms, stables and zoos. He instilled in them his love and respect for animals and his determination to set goals and reach them through hard work and perseverance. On one occasion Fran and Terry recall becoming involved in planting tulip bulbs late into the night by flashlight and not being allowed to quit until all were bedded. One art lesson they received in which Mrs. Boehm was involved (and done without the permission of the landlord) was the painting on one entire wall of a map of the United States—with cities, rivers, mountain ranges, industries, etc. Working evenings, the project took four months to complete. It was a masterpiece.

He taught them how best to sing, talk, walk, dress—every phase of their living received his scrutiny and opinion.

After four years Teresa and Francene graduated and returned home. They visited often, as they still do. The warm, close relationship with Mr. Boehm continued until they began bringing male friends to Trenton; then they noticed a change. Mr. Boehm would be cool to them and their escorts. The girls were no longer in his sphere of influence, no longer needed to rely on him. They had fledged; they had become adults.

A Distributor Is Engaged

On the business front, the responsibilities of covering a market which stretched coast to coast, building an office staff to tend to details of administration, and increasing promotional activities, became too demanding even for Helen Boehm. In order for her to devote more time to the latter two increasingly-important phases, it was determined that a national distributor should be engaged.

On June 1, 1956, Edward Marshall Boehm became associated with Meakin and Ridgway, Inc., of New York City, a

THE WHITE HOUSE
WASHINGTON

October 22, 1957.

PERSONAL

Dear Mr. and Mrs. Boehm:

This note brings you the warm gratitude of Mrs. Eisenhower and myself for the ceramic interpretation of "The Polo Player" that you created for us as a gift to The Queen and Prince Philip. I know that the piece was received with as much pleasure as it gave us to be able to present a porcelain so unique and lovely.

With much admiration of your unusual craftsmanship, and best wishes,

Sincerely,

Dwight D. Eisenhower

Mr. and Mrs. Edward Marshall Boehm,
25 Fairfacts Street,
Trenton 8, New Jersey.

fine firm which for many decades distributed Minton China of England and a few other allied lines. In the early 1960's, Minton, England purchased Meakin and Ridgway, Inc., and the distribution firm was renamed Minton, Inc. Edward Marshall Boehm, Inc., continued the pleasant association until June of 1968 when the studio resumed its own distribution.

The distribution firm, headed by Mr. Bruce Ridgway, later by Mr. John E. Hartill and Mr. Hubert St. Onge, had a staff covering Mrs. Boehm's former territories. Orders and sales steadied and increased and for the first time the Boehms had a "buffer" between themselves and the market to help with merchandising details and problems.

A Royal Gift

The effect of relieving Mrs. Boehm was soon apparent in the promotional area. Learning early in 1957 of an impending visit by Queen Elizabeth and Prince Philip to the United States, and knowing that President and Mrs. Eisenhower would be seeking a fine gift for the Royal Couple, Mrs. Boehm contacted the White House and asked that Mr. Boehm and his art be considered. Mr. Boehm was invited to submit a sketch of a proposed sculpture. Prince Philip on a polo pony was suggested and accepted.

The artist and his staff had four months to prepare the piece. The result, the Polo Player, is a marvel of engineering and artistry. Two-hundred and sixty-eight interlocking mold sections were necessary to cast the piece with the pony in a rearing position (see page 6). At the presentation, October 18 of that year, it was obvious that the royal couple was pleased to receive a gift of porcelain. In a reciprocal, coincidental, but highly-meaningful gesture, Queen Elizabeth and Prince Philip presented President and Mrs. Eisenhower with a Royal Worcester sculpture of birds by Miss Dorothy Doughty. An elegant act of history repeated! The Boehms received their first of many letters from President Eisenhower, shown on opposite page.

That same October of 1957, President Rene Coty of France received from the Marcus family of Dallas (Neiman-Marcus) a pair of Cedar Waxwings. These were given by the President to the Elysée Palace. A beautiful letter of acknowledgment later was received by Mrs. Boehm.

Mrs. Boehm made her first trip out of the country in November, 1957. She conducted an exhibition of porcelains

LE PRÉSIDENT DE LA RÉPUBLIQUE

MENTON, le 3 Janvier 1958.

Madame,

Ils sont remarquables et d'une grâce extrême, ces oiseaux de porcelaine dus au talent de Monsieur BOEHM.

Je vous en remercie d'autant plus vivement qu'ils me seront un nouveau témoignage de l'amitié américaine.

Avec mes sincères félicitations et mes voeux pour 1958, je vous prie d'agréer, Madame, l'expression de mes respectueux hommages.

Madame Helen F. BOEHM
25 Fairfacts Street
TRENTON 8
New-Jersey   U.S.A.

with the fine Canadian firm of Henry Birks & Sons in Montreal. The reception of Canadians to the American porcelains was gratifying and the relationship has remained active ever since.

The following summer President and Mrs. Eisenhower again called on Mr. Boehm for State gifts in preparation for their trip to Canada. On July 9, 1958, the President and First Lady presented Mr. Boehm's Canada Geese and Whippets (see both here) to, respectively, then Governor-General Vincent Massey and Prime Minister John Diefenbaker. In the fall of 1958 these sculptures were acquired by the Royal Ontario Museum in Toronto.

The Smithsonian received its first four important Boehm sculptures in November, 1958, a gift from Mrs. Mary G. Roebling, Chairman of the Board of the Trenton Trust Company, New Jersey. The pieces were Meadowlark, Black-throated Blue Warbler, Yellow-throated Warbler and Percheron Stallion.

Promotional Milestones — Accident And Design

September of 1958 marked one of the rare occasions on which Mr. Boehm ventured from home and work from the time the studio was started. To the amazement of Mrs. Boehm and all who knew him, he responded to an invitation to serve on the

Above: Pair of Canada Geese with goslings

Miss America panel of judges in Atlantic City. At first it appeared that he saw an important promotional opportunity, but this was not the case as he never placed much importance on this phase of the business.

The reason, as he explained, was his life-long attraction to beauty and perfection, and the importance he placed on a selection process. The idea of judging beauty and conformation appealed to him whether the subjects were cows, horses, dogs or people. He completed his judging obligations and returned to serve the following two years as well! Also, in the spring of 1967 he joined the panel of judges in Mobile, Alabama, for the Junior Miss Pageant.

Mrs. Boehm entered a new phase of her work in the fall of 1958. She was invited by the prestigious Congressional Club of Washington, D.C., to present a lecture about her husband and his art. Although frightened by the prospect of appearing before an audience composed of the wives of Congress, the Cabinet and the Supreme Court, the indomitable Helen accepted. Her Italian spirit, enthusiasm and forcefulness carried over into public speaking and, before long, she began receiving invitations from important groups, nationwide, for similar appearances.

One last important episode closed out the exciting year of

Whippet, a large 12 inch by 18 inch one-of-a-kind sculpture

1958—the "Tiffany bird escape." Tiffany and Company, the fine jewelry firm in New York City, included Boehm porcelains in its collections from as early as 1953. Mrs. Boehm would conduct an exhibition there annually, introducing new sculptures and educating patrons to the art. The most memorable of all these exhibitions was that held on October 12, 1958.

Mrs. Boehm and Mrs. Robert Hollensteiner (the former Letitia Baldrige), Publicity Director of Tiffany at the time, decided to stage a show combining porcelain birds with live birds. The source of the birds would be Mr. Boehm's aviaries, assuming Mrs. Boehm was successful in convincing him of the merit of the idea. She was.

The circumstances that followed were too involved to detail here fully. Briefly, many of the exotic tropical birds escaped from Mrs. Boehm's station wagon while unloading at Fifth Avenue and 57th Street, and later also escaped in Tiffany's china and crystal department. The story immediately attracted the press media and the exposure that followed could not have been purchased at any price. Nevertheless, the reaction to his beloved birds' escape by Mr. Boehm, who never admitted to the importance of publicity anyway, may be imagined!

Within two days Mrs. Boehm appeared on the popular Jack Paar and Dave Garroway programs relating her story, at the same time appealing to all to help find and save Mr. Boehm's rare birds (some of which he waited years to acquire!).

News and specialty radio and television stations around the country picked up the story (including Bill Ryan, Arthur Godfrey and Walter Kiernan). Newspapers and wire services had a field day. Two months after the event, Tiffany and Company presented the Boehms with a book full of news clippings from around the world. It was estimated that about six hundred papers carried the story (see page opposite).

Unfortunately, none of the birds was ever recovered, all apparently having perished in that unusually cold October. The response to their plight was heart-warming and overwhelming. More than five thousand persons visited the exhibition that week and telephone calls, letters of sympathy, live pet birds and stuffed models continued to arrive at Tiffany's for weeks afterward.

The "Tiffany bird escape," October 14, 1958

End of the Beginning

As the decade of the 1950's drew to a close, Mr. and Mrs. Boehm were honored by spiritually-rewarding experiences. Early in 1959 Monsignor Emilio A. Cardelia, pastor of Saint Joachim's Parish in Trenton, traveled to Rome for a special audience with His Late Holiness Pope John XXIII. Bearing gifts from his parishioners, Monsignor Cardelia presented the Pope with Mr. Boehm's Cerulean Warblers (see page just below) and a special Crucifix the artist designed for the Parish and Vatican (see page opposite).

Later in the year Mr. Boehm made his first bird-collecting safari to Kenya, Africa. After a stay of about five weeks (during which he collected 161 rare birds), he traveled to Rome where he met Mrs. Boehm. An audience with His Holiness had been arranged and Mr. and Mrs. Boehm spent considerable time with Pope John. Their discussions ranged

Cerulean Warblers

Crucifix

from the sculptures previously presented, to art and its importance to mankind. His Holiness was particularly pleased to learn that like his, Mr. Boehm's background was that of a farmer.

A mishap which occurred during the audience never has been told in previous reports of this experience. This was probably the only time a Pope ever helped pick someone off the floor—Helen Boehm! The fashion of the time called for a tight diameter at the lower terminal of Mrs. Boehm's dress. On meeting His Holiness, she genuflected, tilted because the dress wouldn't give, and fell over sideways at the feet of the Pontiff! As Mr. Boehm would say, "You've heard of the perils of Pauline? This is typical of the hazards of Helen!"

The African safari was the first of several expeditions Mr. Boehm was to make in search of rare birds. He later went to Iceland, Ecuador and New Guinea on collecting trips.

In 1956 Mr. and Mrs. Boehm acquired the present beautiful property located in Washington Crossing, New Jersey. The acreage provided an ideal setting for beautiful gardens and aviaries for which Mr. Boehm long had yearned. By the end of the decade the live bird collection had begun to grow in importance, attracting the attention of ornithologists, zoo directors and nature groups.

The purpose of the expanding bird collection was twofold. The live frame of reference and environment were critical to his work and the work of his staff. In keeping with his sculp-

tures of animals, Mr. Boehm insisted on working from life. As he told one reporter, "You just can't sculpture from a picture or stuffed model. With a picture you don't have the whole bird, only one side or a partial view of it. Few stuffed models are done well. A good taxidermist has to be both an artist and anatomist. Furthermore, one cannot visualize motion, character and expression. You must witness the live bird, and you must carefully and patiently study it."

The second reason for the aviaries was Mr. Boehm's interest in the scientific habits of birds, as with all living things, and in their breeding. He was convinced that, given the proper surroundings and care, most rare birds could, in time, be induced to breed. He proved his point. The Boehm aviaries have probably recorded more first-world breedings of rare species, in the relatively short period of little more than a decade, than any institution.

For a limited time each year, primarily in May when the gardens and birds are at their peak in beauty, the Boehms opened the grounds to invited groups. The first to visit was The Congressional Club (in 1959) before which Mrs. Boehm had presented her lecture the previous year. Since then thousands of nature and bird-loving visitors have enjoyed this beautiful, natural location on the bank of the Delaware River.

*Views of the American Gardens
at the Boehm residence*

By the end of 1959 the character of the porcelain collection was continuing to show rapid change. Many of the non-bird subjects had been discontinued or closed out. Glazing no longer was done, except as needed to increase the effects of realism in pieces (e.g. the grapes of the Cardinals, holly berries of the Black-capped Chickadee).

Mr. Boehm began avoiding private commissions and requests from firms in search of fine promotional pieces (as at the left). He was now programming his work for the future. His goal was to concentrate on birds of America, as did Audubon in two-dimension. Hallmarks were changed to give limited edition sculptures a distinctive identification (see page 263). And, for the first time, Mr. Boehm introduced fine metals in his sculptures to obtain even more freedom and naturalism. The beautiful Eastern Bluebirds (shown opposite), the only limited edition sculpture introduced in 1959, was the first to incorporate this innovation in its stamens.

The end of the decade shows a pause, almost as if taking a second wind, after the long, hard struggle, as the studio redirected itself and Mr. Boehm devoted a good part of his time to developing his garden-aviary complex.

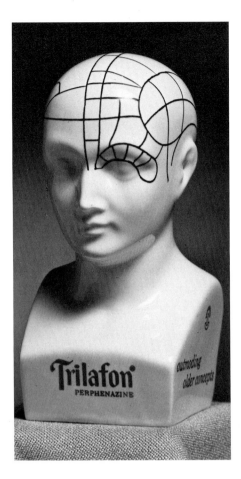

The Phrenology Head—a promotional piece made by Mr. Boehm in the early years of the studio

The Man and The Experience

● *Part III:*
A Decade of Fulfillment—Legacy of Beauty

The second decade of Edward Marshall Boehm's career was to be his last. At the peak of his creative powers, early in the twentieth year of the studio, he suddenly made his transition from life. The date was January 29, 1969. He was fifty-five years of age.

The impact he has made on the art world, in so short a period of creativity, is immense and lasting. As Mr. John E. Hartill stated in his appreciation, "... Edward Marshall Boehm was described as the ceramic genius of the age. In more ways than one he has made ceramic history, and future generations will recognize his work as an important contribution to the art of our time."

Through the nineteen sixties the Boehm art was exported to England, the first American porcelain ever to be sent to Europe. International museum representations increased to

Eastern Bluebirds

twenty-four, with several others planned. And, with three Presidents having received his porcelains during this decade, Mr. Boehm experienced the unique honor of creating sculptures for five American Presidents.

A Tranquil Period

The firm was on solid footing by 1960 and looked to the challenge of the new decade. Relationships with fine galleries and stores were firmly established. The studio staff grew to a total of approximately forty. Demand for some sculptures actually exceeded the capacity of the studio for the first time. Subjects like the Song Sparrows, Carolina Wrens, Cerulean Warblers, Cedar Waxwings, Cardinals, Meadowlark and Red-winged Blackbirds were being accepted in growing numbers by stores and galleries.

Meadowlark

Hunter

Mrs. Boehm and I continued to whittle away at the collection. There were still over a hundred subjects offered, the majority not birds, and the pressure continued to build for more birds. Each cut we made was not without pain to Mr. Boehm. He recognized the sound business reasons for reducing the collection, but he did not find it easy to accept the fact that once subjects were retired it was with the intention of never making them again.

By 1962 the revision was complete. The collection announced contained twenty-five limited edition birds, twenty-one fledgling and non-limited birds, seven religious subjects and two horses (both limited editions, Hunter and Polo Player), a total offering of fifty-five subjects. The collection would remain at approximately this size through ensuing years.

Ruffed Grouse

The pause in new sculptures continued through 1960. Introduced in that year were the Ruffed Grouse only (see just above), a life-sized, handsome pair of male and female. Mr. Boehm continued to be occupied mainly with his burgeoning gardens and aviaries. The live bird population increased to approximately fifteen hundred and most of the eight-and-a-half-acre estate was being utilized.

Mr. and Mrs. Boehm also found themselves devoting an important segment of their time to newspapers, magazines and other media interested in the creative ventures of this talented team. In 1960 three Sunday papers included center-page color spreads in their magazine sections and the Saturday Evening Post ran a magnificent five-page color story in their May issue of that year. Each of these important exposures required time and accommodation. This pattern was repeated in subsequent years but at a somewhat slower pace. Through 1966 it is roughly estimated that the printed publicity attracted by the Boehm experience, if purchased, certainly would have been in excess of a million dollars. This is not including the many radio and television exposures.

In 1961 our late Presidents, Herbert Hoover and John F. Kennedy, were both presented with replicas of Mr. Boehm's proud, white-bisque American Bald Eagle sculpture (see page 91). Mr. Hoover received his from the Explorers Club of New York at a dinner honoring him. This was in April, 1961. The gift pleased him so he wrote Mr. Boehm the letter below.

For his birthday in 1961, President Kennedy was presented with an Eagle by the Democratic Committee of the State of New Jersey.

HERBERT HOOVER

The Waldorf Astoria Towers
New York, New York
April 29, 1961

My dear Mr. Boehm:

In a very busy three days I only today was able to go through your book properly and to have a real look at the eagle.

My admiration for both is unbounded. And, if I may add, my confidence in the future of a great American artist is complete.

With all good wishes,

Yours faithfully,

Herbert Hoover

Mr. Edward Marshall Boehm
25 Fairfacts
Trenton, New Jersey

American Bald Eagle

In October of 1961, during a New Jersey trade mission to
Sweden, then-Governor Robert B. Meyner presented a pair
of Ptarmigan (which were introduced the following spring—
see page 190) to King Gustav VI Adolf. This was one of many
gestures of recognition by the Meyners.

In 1958 they had presented a pair of Mr. Boehm's Cardinals to the New Jersey State Museum and, in 1960, sent a
Chickadee on Holly to the Governors of each state. They
exhibited their private collection in the Governor's mansion
during his tenure. Following his governorship, Mr. Meyner
served as master of ceremonies at two important museum
dedications of Boehm collections. And, Mrs. Meyner not only
attended important exhibitions of Mr. Boehm's art, but later,
as a television personality and columnist, often gave attention
to both Mr. and Mrs. Boehm.

Boldness And Freedom

The collections of 1961 and 1962 began to show increased
sculptural activity, a pattern of metered introductions, and
an emphasis on more important compositions. Three limited
editions were presented each year: in 1961 Sugarbirds, Mockingbirds and Goldfinches; in 1962 Blue Jays, Ptarmigan,
and Lesser Prairie Chickens.

The Sugarbirds are a magnificent, ambitious composition
(see page 189). The piece stands about twenty-six inches tall
and required the making of over four hundred mold sections
for the casting of its fifty-one parts. Four birds (two males,

two females) in different positions surround the stump which is covered with a profusion of ferns, philodendron and orchid plants. The orchid flowers are supported by metal stems.

This sculpture and that of the Mockingbirds (see page 186) introduced another innovation, subjects with removable flowers. Because of the fragility of the orchids and bindweed flowers, with their life-thin construction and freedom, it would have been hazardous to fuse them to the sculptures. Many might be damaged while in transit. By making the flowers removable, they could be shipped separately and later joined to the pieces by placing them into their specially-designed sockets.

The 1961 collection was to be introduced at an exhibition to be held in New York City in the early fall of that year. The Sugarbirds was the last model to be completed and illustrates Mr. Boehm's habit of working up to deadlines and the confidence he possessed as a result of his twelve years of experience with hard-paste.

The one and only Sugarbirds model cast was completely assembled in clay only seven days before the affair. Two and a half of these days would be consumed in the initial bisque firing. Assuming the piece fired perfectly, and the odds certainly were greatly against it as it was the first of this complex sculpture, we would have only four and a half days for the painting and refirings in the color phases.

To add further drama to the situation (a condition in which Mr. Boehm reveled and excelled), Mr. Boehm insisted that the main stump would support itself through the intense heat. Props for this section of the model were not to be used! His key craftsmen protested, as did I. We believed, unanimously, that he was wrong, that the stump needed support. Furthermore, why take the risk? It was a simple matter to add a main prop. Mr. Boehm refused. He was out to prove a point.

The outcome must be obvious. As usual, we were wrong. The Sugarbirds fired perfectly and the main stump moved not at all. With great effort it was painted and refired in the next four-and-a-half days and delivered to New York the day of the exhibition.

The market reaction to the Sugarbirds caught us completely by surprise. Prior to making and distributing replicas we announced to collectors and galleries our intention to make it in a limited edition of fifty. We immediately received a flurry of strong suggestions and protests that an edition of fifty would not satisfy the number of Boehm collectors who would want the piece. In response we issued a new announcement that the Sugarbirds would be made in an edition of one hundred replicas for the world.

The 1962 collection represented a movement away from the popular song-birds to semi-popular and little-known birds. The Ptarmigans are the state bird of Alaska and not seen south of northern Canada; the Prairie Chickens (see page 193) are nearly extinct and are certainly not among the more attractive American birds. And the Blue Jays (see page 194), although beautiful, have few friends among bird-lovers.

"... a bold and independent move ..."

This was a bold and independent move on the part of the artist. Obviously, markets were not a consideration. Mr. Boehm entered a phase where he began to feel that the ornithological importance of portraying with fidelity certain vanishing species such as the Prairie Chickens, and attractive but little-known species like the Ptarmigans, overrode other considerations. In his mind this collection represented one of his most important in terms of accurate depiction and reference for future generations. He knew these birds would not appeal to the majority, the female collectors, and he was partially right. The Prairie Chickens initially attracted the least demand of any subject introduced since 1956; and the Ptarmigans were not received as well as a song-bird would have been.

The Blue Jays, however, proved a sensation from the start. Most people do not like this mischievous, often cruel, bird; but the design and execution are so excellent and "strong" they overcame most criticism and prejudice.

"... a sensation from the start."

Mr. and Mrs. Boehm in their Trenton gallery

The conformation of the Jays, specifically the thin bases, illustrates complete mastery of the hard-paste medium. In studying collections of fine porcelain sculpture, it becomes apparent that most pieces are designed with rather small, round, mounded bases from which the design proceeds in a largely vertical posture. This is because of the great shrinkage and movement in firing. Spherical, vertical shapes are self-supporting, self-compensating, and movement is not so noticeable nor so hazardous in the color firings.

The most difficult shapes to control and fire successfully are squares or rectangles and thin, wide bases like those of the Jays, Cerulean Warblers (see page 82) and Carolina Wrens. In shrinking, these bases tend to draw, warp and curl. In subsequent color firings, uneven heating caused by kiln variation and the joining of thin parts of the models to thick parts, sets up stresses which often result in cracked bases, useless models which must be destroyed.

In spite of the losses and heartaches presented by these and other similar sculptures, Mr. Boehm refused to skirt the issues by simplifying structures, by compromising artistic excellence. "The price must be paid," he said.

"The price must be paid . . ."

Academy to Smithsonian

The earliest comprehensive Boehm collection received by a museum was that given the Academy of Natural Sciences of Philadelphia, the oldest institution of its kind in the country. The gift was from Mr. and Mrs. Morris Gastwirth of New York. At the dedication, May 9, 1963, (see page 96), the donors stated their belief that the naturalistic collection of

the artist was just at home in a natural history museum as it would be in an art museum. Mr. Boehm always considered this one of the highest compliments paid him.

The collection consisted of forty-three subjects, many of them pairs, and included most of the early limited editions: Song Sparrows, Cedar Waxwings, Black-tailed Bantams, Red-winged Blackbirds, Carolina Wrens, Cerulean Warblers, American Eagle, Cardinals, etc. This was the first of the museum dedications to which collectors, business associates and friends were invited. The formal affair was attended by approximately two hundred.

After displaying and caring for the Gastwirth Collection for more than four years, the Trustees of the Academy felt that the art could be enjoyed by so many more if it were housed in a national institution. With the concurrence of the donors, the collection was transferred permanently to the Smithsonian Institution, Washington, D.C., October 5, 1967 (see page opposite).

Extraordinary Sculptures

Like many artists, Mr. Boehm was flamboyant in his promises and overly-generous in giving gifts of his work. It was not uncommon for him to take a piece off display in the gallery and hand it to a youngster or friend. I've seen him do the same in his home with the most prized early porcelains, some of which could not be replaced.

"... flamboyant in his promises ..."

He also had a tendency to give gifts not yet created! A person with whom he felt comfortable might say, "Oh, I'd love to have my collie, 'Baron' done in porcelain." Without hesitation Mr. Boehm might reply, "I'll make him for you," and proceed to do so. Mrs. Boehm and I cringed each time this happened. Not that we weren't in favor of gift-giving, but the creation of a new sculpture, which usually occurred at the most inopportune times, diverted Mr. Boehm's attentions and those of his key artisans from the critical, scheduled work. And he always kept his word.

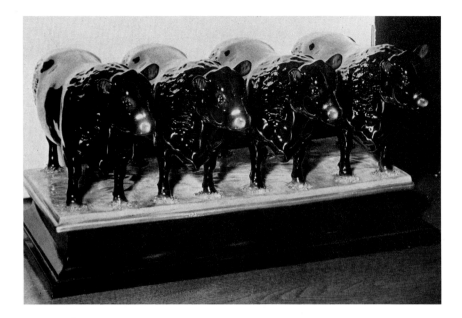

At other times he would conjure ideas of his own for gift-giving. Two occasions of this sort resulted in extraordinarily-beautiful compositions. The first sculpture was done for his friends, Mr. and Mrs. Oliver H. Delchamps, and presented in July, 1963 (see just above). A few years before, one of Mr. Delchamps' Angus cows bore quadruplet calves, all of which survived, an event computed to occur only once in seventeen million births. Each of the calves matured and also had offspring. Mr. Boehm decided an important bovine occurrence of this kind should be recorded in porcelain.

Work on the "quads" began early in 1963, the worst time of the year as we were preparing for our new introductions which usually were presented about May. This unusual sculpture was not ordinary; in fact, many of us doubted that four porcelain Angus figures could be fired simultaneously on one thin, flat base. The project intrigued Mr. Boehm and he gave more attention to it than he did to the new bird sculptures.

By July the quads were finally successfully fired, but not until several models broke while in the greenware stage. Two either had collapsed or curled in the bisque firing and one other, after painting, cracked through the thin base in the decorated kiln.

A second magnificent piece resulted from an invitation sent by Mr. Stanley Marcus inviting Mr. Boehm to decorate an Easter Egg. This was early in 1966 when Neiman-Marcus, in a drive to raise monies for the annual Easter Seals campaign, sent white eggs to well-known personalities all over the country with a letter asking all to decorate the eggs in imaginative fashion and return them to Dallas. The eggs were

"... extraordinarily
beautiful
compositions ..."

to be entered in a well-publicized auction.

The egg sent by Neiman-Marcus was large, poorly shaped and made of plaster-of-paris. Mr. Boehm took one look at it and said, "I certainly won't put my name to that thing; we'll make them a real egg!" The problem was that only two weeks remained before the auction, three days of which had to be allowed for shipping; and, making an egg that shows no seams is extremely difficult to do in hard-paste porcelain.

For ten days Mr. Boehm had the studio virtually turned upside-down. All key artisans were involved and kilns were held up in order to have them standing by and ready. The egg was completed (see page 100) and reached Dallas in time.

Collectors had heard of the intense struggle going on in Trenton and attended the auction. The magnificent egg brought approximately 50 per cent of the total proceeds.

"Carrying Coals to Newcastle"

In the fall of 1963 Mrs. Boehm made a two-week visit to

Below: At the New Jersey State Museum, Trenton, New Jersey, May 7, 1966. From left: Mr. Boehm; Mr. Athelstan Caröe (Chairman of Minton China, England); Mrs. Boehm; and Mr. and Mrs. Oliver H. Delchamps. The Delchamps presented a collection of Mr. Boehm's porcelains to the Museum.

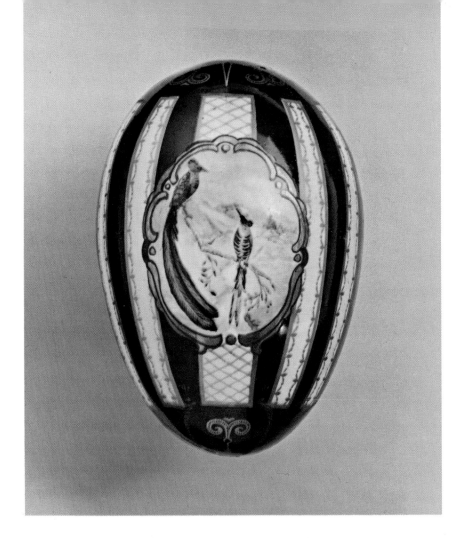

London, England, specifically to determine whether Mr. Boehm's art might be accepted by one or two of the fine galleries there. She felt it was time we shared some of Mr. Boehm's art with our distant friends, and she was also aware that no American porcelain ever had been exported to important European cradles of the art form. It would be prestigious for America and Mr. Boehm and his artisans if she found acceptance of the porcelains in London.

To her great pleasure and surprise, Mr. Boehm's art and reputation had long preceded her. Each of the five fine stores and galleries she visited were eager for an association and representation of the collection. Furthermore, she was told that the porcelain studios and factories, as well, were familiar with Mr. Boehm's art and techniques and that his progress was carefully studied in England.

She faced the dilemma of selecting one representative from the five. Mr. Boehm had not been in favor of the trip nor its purpose. His comment was, "Why are you going out of the country when we are not even meeting the demand here?" As stated previously, Mr. Boehm never gave much importance to matters of prestige or promotion!

The two stores which Mrs. Boehm most liked were Thomas Goode and Company and Asprey and Company. Both were

One side of ornate egg with double-sided "Bird-of-Paridise" design

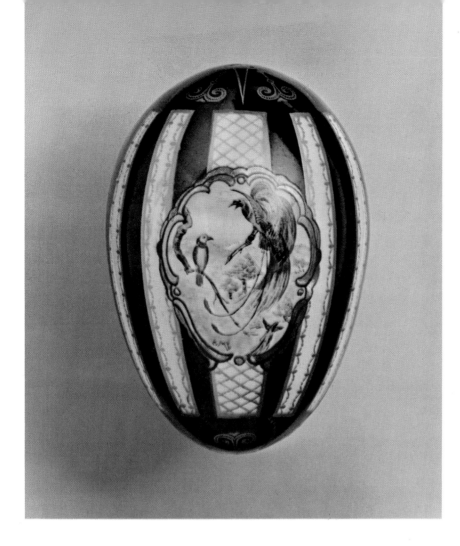

world-known, of the highest quality and refinement, yet were different in character and presentation. Unable to choose between them, Mrs. Boehm held a meeting with principals of both and offered representations to both if they would agree to hold an initial exhibition jointly. It was like asking two fine, independent stores in the United States to do a show together! Mrs. Boehm held her breath, but not for long. The principals agreed and an exhibition date was set for the following summer, June 23, 1964.

Preparations for the important London exhibition had to be made well in advance. Initially Mr. Boehm showed no interest in the event; but as the weeks passed and he learned that the finest English porcelain makers would be represented at the exhibition, he realized that for the image of "Boehm" and America it would be important that we make a lasting impression.

The Ivory-Billed Woodpeckers

Apart from the collection being sent to London, something spectacular had to be done. In January of 1964 it was decided that we would create one of the largest sculptures ever in hard-paste porcelain. The subject selected was the supposedly-

Opposite side of ornate egg

extinct Ivory-billed Woodpeckers whose wing-span measured up to twenty-seven inches across. The sketch showed the male bird in flight about to land on the top of a stump. He would be supported by a thick branch. Midway on the stump the female Woodpecker would be giving her attentions to a youngling whose head would protude from its nest-hole. At the bottom of the stump a turtle would be straining its neck to see what the ruckus above was all about. The piece would have to be completed in five months. Its estimated weight, when fired, would be a hundred pounds.

The sizes and positions of the Woodpeckers dictated a total composition which would stand approximately five feet tall. Major problems were ahead in the molding, casting and firing, all of which constitute reasons why ceramists avoid large subjects. The sculpture would be dissected into components, but major components, particularly the male bird wings and main stump parts, would require large, heavy molds. Once a mold reaches such proportions and weight that a single caster no longer can handle it alone, the sensitivity and feel are lost.

To have enough absorption potential to make a satisfactory casting, a mold must have at least ten times the volume of the casting. This is why some of the Woodpecker molds weighed between two hundred and four hundred pounds. The total weight of all molds for the sculpture was approximately three thousand pounds. Four artisans were needed to cast the larger sections.

Casting the major part of the stump and the male wings was a frustrating experience. In order for the clay to support itself, the stump had to be cast three-quarters of an inch thick. This took about three hours of setting-up during which time the mold had to be turned constantly so the thickening cast would be relatively uniform. After several tries we were successful.

We began casting the male wings one Friday morning. This stretched into Sunday night before we had our first success. Mr. Boehm refused to quit until we had a perfect cast. A couple of the artisans had only a few hours sleep through this trying experience. At least two dozen attempts were made before success. The additional problem here was the removal of the wing and wing feathers as a unit from the mold. The individual feathers were as long as seven inches and so thin they refused to remain intact when separated from the mold.

Eventually we had several successful castings of the sculpture. All went well through other stages until the first

Ivory-billed Woodpeckers

June 13, 1964

Her Majesty,
Queen Elizabeth 11
London, England

Your Majesty,

The Congressional Club was privileged last week to have a preview of the Porcelain Art of Edward Marshall Boehm that is being shown in London on June 23rd at the London-Hilton.

Since this is the first time American porcelain has been shown on foreign shores...we thought it appropriate that you have a first look at the latest achievement done by this world famous artist.

The Congressional Club is composed of the wives of the United States Congress, the Supreme Court and Cabinet of the United States.

Because the robin and the daffodil are so typically American, we have chosen this particular Porcelain sculpture to send to you with all good wishes for your continued happiness and well-being.

Respectfully yours,

Carrie Davis

Mrs. Clifford Davis
President, The Congressional Club

P.S. The package is being mailed air-express on June 15th.

decorated firing (conducted in the bisque kiln because the decorating kilns were too small to accommodate the piece). Although the rise in temperature to anneal the colors was slow (about eight hours), it was too rapid and the piece cracked into many pieces. Color firings of the second model were slowed down considerably and we finally had our first completed Ivory-billed Woodpeckers sculpture (see page 103).

A Bon Voyage

As with other important events, word of the large sculpture and the London exhibition was quick to spread. To the great pleasure of Mr. and Mrs. Boehm a telephone call came from Mrs. Clifford Davis, President of The Congressional Club, inviting Mrs. Boehm to exhibit the Ivory-billed Woodpeckers and the rest of the collection for the club members just prior to the departure for England.

Invitations announced the world-premiere showing of the sculpture in Washington, D.C., June 4, 1964. By now the members had become knowledgeable about the Boehms and their work. The club overflowed with well-wishers, a fitting tribute to the artist and his staff and to American art.

A further expression of the Congressional Club's pleasure and pride was their decision to send a gift of Mr. Boehm's porcelain to The Queen to mark the first exportation of American porcelain. This ranks as one of the greatest honors ever

8th August, 1964.

Dear Mr. Clifford Davis,

I am commanded by The Queen to
send you this expression of Her Majesty's
sincere thanks for your kindness in having
sent her the very beautiful porcelain robin,
and also the interesting book, by Edward
Marshall Boehm.

Her Majesty is delighted to have
this ornament and book, and would be grateful
if you would convey an expression of her
gratitude and appreciation to the Members of
the Congressional Club, who joined with you
in sending The Queen these charming gifts.

Yours sincerely
Martin Charteris

Mrs. Clifford Davis,
   President,
      The Congressional Club.

accorded the Boehms. Mrs. Davis called the Robin selected (see page 202) a "gift from all Americans." It truly was. A letter from Mrs. Davis accompanied the gift, and a reply, at the command of Queen Elizabeth, was received.

The promotional arrangements for the trip were thorough and imaginative as are all of Mrs. Boehm's projects. She decided to take the French liner S.S. France to Southampton and to have exhibitions and film showings on both legs of the trip. The French Line agreed and made every effort to accommodate Mrs. Boehm and her birds. All details were covered including literature printed in French, invitations to all passengers, and "Boehm" menus for a special dinner held by the Captain.

A Royal Welcome

When Mrs. Boehm reached Southampton she was greeted by representatives of Thomas Goode and Company and Asprey and Company, Messrs. Philip B. Rayner and Eric Asprey. A large van was on hand to carry the collection. The Woodpeckers sculpture was packed in a wooden crate which measured three feet wide, three feet deep and six feet high. Surrounding and protecting the sculpture was popcorn, lots of popcorn, ready to cascade and engulf those who would unpack the piece.

The exhibition was held at the London Hilton in three adjoining rooms. The main area contained the collection exhibited as one would use art pieces in a home. English antique tables, sideboards and mantles elegantly complimented the art. The second room was for refreshments; the third was turned into a small theater for continuous film showings.

Highlight of the opening of the exhibition was the appearance of a member of the Royal Family, The Honorable Angus Ogilvy, husband of Princess Alexandra. Mrs. Boehm was given the pleasure of escorting Mr. Ogilvy about the collection. The subject he admired most, both for its sculptural form and color, was the Blue Jays. His comment was that "Americans surely must love so beautiful a bird." Mrs. Boehm did not reply.

The Presidential Eagle

During her stay in London, Mrs. Boehm visited the United States Embassy to tell them about the exhibition and the porcelains. While meeting with officials she suggested that an American Eagle, exactly like the one presented to our late President John F. Kennedy in 1961, be permanently exhibited in the Embassy in honor and memory of Mr. Kennedy. The officials accepted the suggestion with enthusiasm. A presentation date was set for September 14, 1964. Mrs. Boehm returned to London with the eagle. Our Ambassador, Mr. David Bruce, accepted the eagle for the Embassy and in behalf of Mr. Kennedy's family (see page 106).

Exhibition In Retrospect

Early in 1963 Mr. Reese Palley of the Gallery Reese Palley, Atlantic City, a representative of Boehm porcelains for many years, told us of an ambitious plan to stage a retrospective exhibition the following year with the intention of showing one of each of Mr. Boehm's sculptures made to date. The opening of the exhibition was to be August 25, 1964, and would coincide with the Democratic National Convention to be held in Atlantic City at that time.

The planning had begun so far in advance because of the immense task of accumulating from widely diverse sources approximately three hundred porcelain subjects. Mr. Palley also intended to catalogue the collection by subject name, identification number, description, dimensions, and the number of each subject made. We cooperated to the extent of the early subjects we have, but this amounted to only approximately half of the total collection. The rest would have to be located and borrowed from private collectors.

By August of 1964 all but a handful of the total collection was in Atlantic City and the catalogue was completed. On the 25th of that month, Mrs. Richard J. Hughes, wife of the Governor of New Jersey, officially opened the exhibition. Through the next month and a half, the length of time the collection was shown, most Boehm collectors and friends from all over the country attended the exhibition.

Three months prior to the exhibition, Governor and Mrs. Hughes introduced President and Mrs. Lyndon B. Johnson to Mr. Boehm's art by presenting them with a pair of Mockingbirds, the State bird of Texas (see page 108). The occasion was a State Democratic Committee Dinner held in Atlantic City May 9, 1964.

Balanced Collections

Limited edition sculptures, introduced from 1963 through 1966, represented relatively balanced collections. The 1963 issues were Mearns' Quail, Mountain Bluebirds and Towhee. The Quail (see page 196) are rare southwestern game birds. It was difficult for Mr. Boehm to obtain live ones for models, but he did. The porcelain pair is a good example of excellent

*Governor
Richard J. Hughes
of New Jersey
presents a pair
of Mr. Boehm's
"Mockingbirds"
(State bird
of Texas) to
President and Mrs.
Lyndon B. Johnson,
Atlantic City,
May 9, 1964.*

hand-painting on porcelain.

The Mountain Bluebirds (see page 198) were designed as a centerpiece for Mrs. Boehm. She had long wanted an important composition which could be used in lieu of flowers. One of this edition later was presented by the Democratic Leadership of Congress to Captain Charles S. Robb and Lynda Bird Johnson as a wedding gift, December, 1967.

Topping the 1964 collection was the Robin with daffodils, joined by a pair of Killdeer with young and a Bobolink. The Robin, previously mentioned as having been selected as a gift for Queen Elizabeth, was one of the most popular of all Boehm sculptures. It was used for other important gifts including that given by President Richard Nixon to His Holiness Pope Paul VI in March, 1969 (see page opposite).

In 1965 five limited editions were presented: Fledgling Great Horned Owl, Varied Buntings, Tufted Titmice, Catbird, and Parula Warblers. This was a diversified collection. Structurally important is the Varied Buntings (see page 210). At the top of a metal stem is an umbrellic cluster of six Crown Imperial flowers and three buds. The sensitive bright orange coloring of the flowers is among the most difficult we have had to contend with in the decorated kiln. The Owl was a popular subject in this collection. In March of 1966 Prince Philip of Great Britain was presented with an Owl during a visit to New York City.

President Richard Nixon presents Mr. Boehm's "Robin with Daffodils"
to His Holiness, Pope Paul VI, The Vatican, March 2, 1969.

Wood Thrushes with azaleas were introduced in 1966 along with a pair of Green Jays and the Rufous Hummingbirds. In intricacy and floral beauty the Thrushes surpassed all prior sculptures. Construction of the pair required the making of over six hundred mold sections. The twenty-eight long, slender wild azaleas contain one hundred and sixty-eight hand-fashioned metal stems and stamens.

The Wood Thrushes were involved in an event that drew much good-natured attention in Washington, D.C., the early part of 1967. Mrs. Boehm had learned that our nation's capital and the District of Columbia did not have an "official bird." For approximately forty years the Wood Thrush was their "unofficial bird." To rectify this, and with the help of a good friend, Mr. Ralph Becker, of Washington, Mrs. Boehm initiated action to have the Thrush made official. The Audubon Society, Commissioners and Historical Society were fully informed of the situation.

The Thrush finally was made official and the press learned of the high-level decision. Reporters had great fun lampooning local politicians for demeaning the Thrush and for having kept it "illegitimate" for so long a period. In tribute to the bird, and to call attention to its overdue election, a pair of Mr. Boehm's porcelain Wood Thrushes were placed on permanent display in the Commissioners' Building in Washington. Mrs. Boehm attended the presentation ceremony, February 27, 1967 (see page 110).

Collections For Posterity

Gifts of important private collections to museums and art centers continued in the 1960's. On May 7, 1966, three years after the Gastwirth gift to Philadelphia, Mr. and Mrs. Oliver H. Delchamps honored Mr. Boehm and his artisans by presenting sixty-two sculptures to the New Jersey State Museum, Trenton. The dedication was attended by approximately three hundred collectors and friends (see page 99). Mr. Robert B. Meyner officiated at the formal proceedings.

The Arkansas Arts Center received permanent loan of a collection of fifty-six sculptures, provided by Mr. and Mrs. Raymond Rebsamen of Little Rock. The dedication was held November 22, 1966 (shown below). Included in the collection are: Song Sparrows, Cedar Waxwings, Black-tailed Bantams, Red-winged Blackbirds, Cerulean Warblers, Carolina Wrens and Eastern Bluebirds. The collection is uniquely displayed in a glass-walled, rectangular room which allows the porcelains to be viewed from an outside courtyard.

In 1967, three comprehensive collections were received by widely-separated institutions. In early February of that year Mr. and Mrs. Ned Mudge of Dallas, Texas, began giving

Below left: Mr. and Mrs. Ned Mudge of Dallas, Texas, with Mr. Hal P. Kirby, Director of the Dallas Museum of Natural History. In 1967 the Mudges began giving an important collection of Boehm porcelains to the Museum.

Below right: Mrs. Boehm with Mr. and Mrs. Raymond Rebsamen and their grandson, Raymond Remmel, at the Arkansas Arts Center, Little Rock, November 22, 1966. The Rebsamens presented the Center a permanent loan of fifty-six Boehm sculptures.

ownership of their great collection to the Dallas Museum of Natural History (see page 111).

March 9, 1967, marked the dedication of a gift to the famous Bellingrath Gardens (the Bellingrath-Morse Foundation) near Mobile, Alabama. This was presented by the Delchamps family—Oliver H. Delchamps, Alfred Delchamps and their sister, Mrs. Wayne S. Moore. The initial gift consisted of sixty-seven subjects. Since then Mr. and Mrs. Oliver H. Delchamps have added, on permanent loan, additional subjects which have brought the total to in excess of eighty. All of the rare, early porcelains are represented including a Golden Pheasant, one of only seven Mr. Boehm made in color.

The dedication was attended by approximately three hundred and fifty guests. Again Mr. Robert B. Meyner accepted an invitation to be master of ceremonies.

Mr. and Mrs. Boehm had visited the Bellingrath Gardens and Home on a prior trip to Mobile. The exquisite setting provides so natural a background for the porcelains that they decided to add a sculpture of the Ivory-billed Woodpeckers to the Bellingrath Gardens collection.

At a dinner party the night following the Bellingrath dedication, Dr. and Mrs. Samuel Lombardo of Jacksonville, Florida, and Mr. and Mrs. Oliver Delchamps announced to their friends and guests their intention of presenting a collection to the John F. Kennedy Center for the Performing

The Bellingrath dedication, March 9, 1967, Mobile, Alabama From left: Mr. George Downing; Mr. Boehm; and Mr. Oliver H. Delchamps. A collection of Mr. Boehm's art was presented to the Bellingrath-Morse Foundation by the Delchamps and Moore families of Mobile.

Arts, the construction of which had begun in Washington, D.C. They estimated the collection would approximate that given Bellingrath. Mr. Ralph Becker, General Counsel of the Center, was present to represent the Center and to act as liaison.

The gift was accepted December 6, 1967, in Trenton, New Jersey, by Mr. Roger L. Stevens, then Chairman of the John F. Kennedy Center and of the National Council On The Arts (see just above).

Other institutions which received partial collections during the 1960's included: Ha'aretz Museum (Tel Aviv, Israel), Birmingham Museum of Art (Alabama), Louisiana Arts and Science Center (Baton Rouge), The Herron Museum (Indianapolis), and the Santa Fe Museum (New Mexico).

Duncravin Farm

In June of 1964, Mr. and Mrs. Boehm purchased a farm in Harbourton, New Jersey, only three miles from their home. This was to provide a great source of pleasure for Edward Boehm. In the five years to follow he would build one of the greatest herds of Holstein ever assembled, accumulate a string of horses (saddle and standardbred), breed fancy fowl, and bring together a great tropical fish collection.

A good part of his time was occupied with farm projects. Beautiful new barns were built for the animals, including a

Above from left: Mr. Oliver H. Delchamps, Mobile, Alabama; Mr. Roger L. Stevens, Chairman of The John F. Kennedy Center For The Performing Arts and of the National Council On The Arts; Mr. Boehm; and Dr. Samuel S. Lombardo, Jacksonville, Florida, shown at the Boehm Gallery, Trenton, New Jersey, December 6, 1967. The Delchamps and Lombardos jointly presented a collection of Mr. Boehm's art to the John F. Kennedy Center.

"Golden Thunderbolt," one of Mr. Boehm's prized stallions

milking barn, all driveways were landscaped and lighted, and quarters were built for the managers. The farm is a show place incorporating the best elements of Early American design.

Mrs. Boehm assumed the farm identification would bear the name of Edward Marshall Boehm. Not so. Mr. Boehm named it "Duncravin." At first the significance of this name escaped us all. He later explained it was formed by a combination of two words, "done craving." A life-long dream finally had been realized; Edward Marshall Boehm had his own farm.

Edward and Helen Boehm with "Duncravin Royal Successor,"
"King's Arctic Rose's" bull calf, at the Boehm farm in
August 1968. Successor is now standing at Curtiss Breeding
Service, Inc., Cary, Illinois.

Duncravin
Farms

Left: One of four Jersey
cows Mr. Boehm presented
Mrs. Boehm as her Christmas
gift in 1966.

Lower left (opposite page):
"Matador Heckettier 134"
of Mr. Boehm's Angus herd.
In the spring of 1969 Mrs.
Boehm presented Matador to
Rutgers University.

The Year 1968

The beginning of 1968 was largely devoted to coordinating Boehm Gallery openings with fine stores representing the collection. The most publicized was in San Francisco. Mr. Reese Palley acquired a famous gallery on Maiden Lane designed by the late Frank Lloyd Wright. It would be used to house a comprehensive collection of porcelain by Edward Marshall Boehm. The structure, considered one of Mr. Wright's finest creations, served as the prototype for his Guggenheim Museum. Mrs. Ronald Reagan, wife of the Governor of California (collectors of Mr. Boehm's art), opened the gallery May 30.

Later in the year Mrs. Reagan invited Mrs. Boehm, in cooperation with Bullocks Wilshire, Los Angeles, to exhibit a collection at the Republican Governors' Conference to be held in Palm Springs, California, the beginning of December. On the sixth of that month a luncheon was held about the pool at the palatial home of Mr. George Hearst, Sr. Mr. Boehm's limited editions were used as centerpieces on the tables. With Mrs. Boehm present, Mrs. Reagan presented a Baby Wood Thrush to each of the thirty-two governors' wives and to Mrs. Spiro Agnew, wife of our Vice President (see above).

Above at left is Mrs. Boehm with Mrs. Walter Annenberg and at right with Mrs. Spiro Agnew at the home of Mr. George Hearst, Sr., Republican Governors' Conference, Palm Springs, California, December 6, 1968.

The Final Collections

The porcelain collections of 1967, 1968, 1969 and 1970 continued to show an evolution of the skills of Edward Marshall Boehm and his artisans. Bird subjects selected range the spectrum of American species.

With the exception of the Crested Flycatcher, a subject admired both for the artistry and balance of the sweetgum setting (see page 224), the 1967 collection was modest in size, but not in intricacy. The Fledgling Canada Warbler (see page 231) captivated all who saw it. For the first time a hand-pierced base was introduced; and the technically-difficult task of creating a realistic, life-sized Monarch butterfly was achieved. A Blue Grosbeak and Northern Water-thrush completed the collection.

The sizes and characters of the birds in the 1968 collection were in sharp contrast to the prior year's models. Those selected are unique birds, only one is well-known, but all are excellent sculptural subjects. The most desired, as indicated by the subsequent reactions of collectors, are the Common Tern, and the popular Road Runner. The latter was long in coming. At first Mr. Boehm was not interested in the Road Runner; but after several years of often-repeated requests for it, he finally acceded. The Mergansers and Kestrels, also introduced in 1968, were his personal favorites of the four. (Mr. Boehm often disagreed with the consensus about his work. Among his favorites were some of the less popular pieces, including Green Jays, Downy Woodpeckers, Prairie Chickens, and Parula Warblers.)

"... his personal favorites ..."

The 1969 collection was introduced posthumously. A selection of six sculptures was presented. For the first time in many years, the collection varied in subject matter. Included were: Western Bluebirds with yellow azaleas, Verdins with Stewart Crucifixion-thorn, Black-headed Grosbeak with vine maple, Young American Bald Eagle, a horse ("Adios"), and a pair of glazed figurines called "Beau Brummells."

The Bluebirds (see page 243), as described in the chapter about the process, is more complicated and detailed than the Wood Thrushes. The Eaglet (see page 240) was designed by Mr. Boehm for the incoming President as a symbol of vigor, determination and faith in our youth. The first of this sculpture was presented to President Nixon in the summer of 1969.

"... a symbol of vigor ..."

Adios was modeled after a great horse Mr. Boehm ad-

117

mired. He was the most successful of all equine sires and, during his lifetime, 1940 to 1965, contributed greatly to the sport of harness racing. Mr. Boehm also respected the close relationship that existed between Adios and his owners, Mr. and Mrs. Delvin Miller of Washington, Pennsylvania. He designed the piece as a gift to the Millers and presented the first model to them in October, 1968, as shown above.

Glazed figurines were out of character with the artist's work of the preceding fifteen years. This was intentional. As with Adios, Mr. Boehm had decided he occasionally would move away from birds in subject matter. He wanted to show his versatility and that of his staff. The Beau Brummell style of dress was rich and elegant, affording an opportunity to reintroduce brilliant, royal colors to his porcelain; and he wished once again to present his beautiful, water-clear glaze.

The first sculpture to be introduced in the beginning of 1970 was the Edward Marshall Boehm Orchid Centerpiece (see page 253), a profusion of orchids and hummingbirds. Early in 1968 the Rod McLellan Company of San Francisco, world's largest growers of orchids, asked if they might name a new orchid after Mr. Boehm. The request pleased Mr. Boehm. Having a living thing named after him was important and perpetual. He was invited to select the orchid he most liked from a collection of several new varieties that were to be sent to him.

Mr. and Mrs. Boehm present the first sculpture of "Adios," champion sire of all breeds, to Mr. and Mrs. Delvin Miller of Washington, Pennsylvania, former owners of the horse, at the Boehm farm, October 14, 1968.

Receiving the orchid varieties proved to be an upsetting experience. The first shipment, which contained twenty-four beautiful blooms, each in its own vial, did not arrive the day it should have. It was held over enroute and stored in a baggage room without heat. When we finally located and received the flowers, all had been frozen.

This kind of error, which Mr. Boehm insisted was caused by carelessness, repeated a situation experienced many times in the past with rare bird shipments. I've never seen him more furious. Every baggage manager and executive up to the president of the airline felt the wrath of Edward Boehm. A second shipment was sent and arrived in perfect condition. The airline executives had alerted their men down the line to look for and expedite Mr. Boehm's orchids!

Four other limited edition sculptures completed by Mr. Boehm were introduced in 1970: Oven Bird, a second pair of Beau Brummells, Orchard Oriole, and an important marine sculpture. This latter composition, named "Fondo Marino," is probably the most intricate hard-paste porcelain ever made. In total mold parts it is approximately triple that of the Western Bluebirds.

"... the most intricate ever made."

Future Plans

Edward Marshall Boehm was a man of the future. With all projects, including his art, his interest waned once the result was in sight, once "the corner had been turned." His thoughts and plans were far ahead of us, in many directions at once; and he was restless, impatient to begin new projects. In serious discussion with him, time after time he would say, "There is so much I want to do; I only hope I'm given enough time to do it."

At the time of his transition from life, he had begun plans for creative ventures he said "would turn the art world on its ear." The porcelain art would remain most important to him, but he knew he had controlled and mastered it to a point that would allow him to put some of his time and energies into other artistic endeavors.

"... would turn the art world on its ear."

In the fall of 1968 he had gas lines brought to the studio and began installing glass kilns. For a year he worked with Rutgers University on plans to make art glass and crystal. He was fascinated with these media. He felt, for example, that much finer crystal paperweights could be made than are being made presently; and he wanted to make exquisite

crystal service plates, imbedding into the bases of the plates life-like, colored porcelain inlays of fish and birds.

For years he had worked sporadically on bird designs for porcelain dinnerware. He actually completed a selection of finished prototype plates which he hoped one day to produce. As with crystal he felt there was a need for good bird patterns, that birds in flight postures lent themselves particularly well to the decoration of tablewares. At this writing the Lenox Company is preparing to introduce the first of Mr. Boehm's dinnerware designs (see page 182).

He also devoted considerable time to the design of new porcelain subject lines; framed, hand-painted porcelain wall plaques with bird and flower designs in flat and in bas-relief and models of pieces combining porcelain, ormolu and vermeil. This encompasses the unfinished work of Edward Marshall Boehm—tremendous in scope, creative in conception, vital, as is all good art. Had Mr. Boehm known he would not have the opportunity to accomplish these goals, or at least a good part of

"Golden-crowned Kinglets," designed by Edward Boehm and his artisans, a dinnerware pattern for future introduction

120

Boehm service plate with demi-tasse cup and saucer, Made in 1950

At upper left on opposite page and below right, a pair of handpainted porcelain plaques— "Goldfinches" (unfinished) and "Purple Finches"— designed by Mr. Boehm and his artisans

them, he would have felt cheated and immensely disappointed. To him the porcelain venture of the last two decades was just a beginning, a point of departure. To the world of the present, and the future, it is infinitely more.

Perpetuity

The decision to continue the work of Edward Marshall Boehm had long before been made by Mr. Boehm. On several occasions he told Mrs. Boehm and me, jointly and individually, that the firm must be continued after he was gone. He mentioned it again only about a week before he was suddenly stricken. He knew the traditions and techniques established with his key artisans were good and important and had to be perpetuated. It remained only for Mrs. Boehm to announce the decision to all, which she did in subsequent weeks.

A fitting tribute was paid Mr. Boehm by President Nixon immediately after Mr. Boehm's transition. He and Mrs. Nixon were familiar with Mr. Boehm's birds from the time of

Mockingbird plaques, handpainted on porcelain.
Introduced in 1970

The first pair of a series designed by Mr. Boehm
and his artisans

OFFICE OF THE VICE PRESIDENT
WASHINGTON

June 5, 1959

Dear Mr. and Mrs. Boehm:

Mrs. Nixon and I enjoyed our brief but pleasant visit with you at the Congressional Club reception. We only wish we could have talked longer with you about the justly-famed Boehm porcelain and had an opportunity to express more fully our great appreciation for the special pieces you were kind enough to bring for us.

You may be sure the beautiful California quails found a warm welcome at our house. All of us are proud indeed to own these fine examples of American artistry and craftsmanship. We shall always prize your handsome pair of birds in our home and they will often remind us of your generous and friendly thoughts.

With our appreciation and best wishes to both of you,

Sincerely,

Richard Nixon

Richard Nixon

Mr. and Mrs. Edward Boehm
25 Fairfacts Street
Trenton, New Jersey

THE WHITE HOUSE
WASHINGTON

September 2, 1969

Dear Mrs. Boehm:

Thank you for your recent letter and the photographs of the porcelain Boehm birds you have so generously donated to the White House.

On behalf of the Committee for the Preservation of the White House it is an honor for me to accept these unique examples of your late husband's work for the White House Collection. Although former First Families have enjoyed Mr. Boehm's porcelains in their private collections, not until now has his genius been permanently represented in the White House. We are deeply grateful for your most exquisite gift.

To complete the formal acknowledgement of this important gift, you may expect to receive a letter and engraved certificate of acceptance from the National Park Service on behalf of the Nation in the near future.

With deep appreciation, and with all good wishes,

Sincerely,

James R. Ketchum

James R. Ketchum
Curator

Mrs. Edward Marshall Boehm
25 Fairfacts Street
Trenton, New Jersey 08638

---

his Vice Presidency. In fact, Mr. and Mrs. Boehm had met the Nixons as early as 1959. The Congressional Club held a luncheon reception for Vice President and Mrs. Nixon in May of that year, an event to which the Boehms were invited. This was another of the few invitations Mr. Boehm accepted. During the luncheon the Nixons received as a gift a pair of Mr. Boehm's California Quail. Mr. Nixon sent a letter of thanks.

On February 12, 1969, Mrs. Boehm received a call from President Nixon's office. The President was planning his first European trip, a tour of several countries, and he expressed a desire to present gifts of Mr. Boehm's birds to foreign dignitaries of those countries. The presentations were:

His Excellency Harold Wilson of Great Britain—Tern.

His Excellency Heinrich Luebke of West Germany—Kestrels.

His Excellency Mariano Rumor of Italy—Catbird.

His Excellency Maurice Couve de Murville—Mountain Bluebirds.

His Holiness Pope Paul VI—Robin.

The week after his return from Europe, in March, President Nixon presented a sculpture of the Flycatcher to visiting Prime Minister Pierre Elliott Trudeau of Canada.

In the summer of 1969 Mrs. Boehm presented a selection of ten of Mr. Boehm's most important bird sculptures to the White House for its permanent collection. On August 21, the day Mr. Boehm would have marked his fifty-sixth birthday, Mrs. Boehm personally placed the sculptures in President Nixon's office, the Oval Room. The letter of acknowledgement received from Mr. James R. Ketchum, Curator of the White House, appears at left.

While in the process of announcing plans for continuation of Mr. Boehm's art, Mrs. Boehm sent a letter informing President Nixon of the decision. His reply speaks for all who are aware of the contributions of Edward Marshall Boehm; and it serves as a fitting point of departure for those of us, Mrs. Boehm and his staff, who are privileged to continue his lessons of excellence.

THE WHITE HOUSE

WASHINGTON

April 11, 1969

Dear Mrs. Boehm:

I was very pleased to learn through your April 8
letter that you have decided to carry on your
husband's outstanding work. The many people
all over the world who have admired his art will,
I am sure, regard your decision as an outstanding
and appropriate tribute to his memory. I want you
to know that I greatly appreciate your thoughtfulness
in letting me know of your plans for the future.

With my best wishes,

Sincerely,

Richard Nixon

Mrs. Edward Marshall Boehm
25 Fairfacts Street
Trenton, New Jersey 08638

Edward Marshall Boehm was a fascinating and talented personality with many levels of mood, activity and comprehension. A biographical narrative would not fathom his full essence and character; nor would it define precisely the substance of his art. At best it will provide a thorough introduction to the artist and his contribution.

Each collector and student of Mr. Boehm's art will form his own image of the man. Each will become involved in his own way.

In the following pages a series of vignettes is presented. These have been collected from Mrs. Boehm and from the artist's closest friends and associates. Through them I hope each reader better may render his own portrait of Edward Marshall Boehm.

The MAN
in vignettes . . .

Bringing Birds To Safety

Mr. Boehm's bird-trapping safaris were exceptionally fruitful and successful; but information about his trips to New Guinea, Iceland and Africa is sparse as he never cared to give much detail. The only complete report we received was following his trip to Ecuador in February of 1961. A good friend, Bernard Moos, went with him and kept notes on the daily activities.

As with his other trips, all birds from Ecuador were brought back live and in good strength. The collection comprised sixty-three beautiful specimens. The main ingredients in bringing birds in successfully, according to Mr. Boehm, were proper conditioning before shipment and good care and feeding during transit.

While in flight he would travel right with his birds and would not allow them to be placed in the cold, dark holds of cargo planes. After the return from Ecuador, Mr. Moos told the following story. "The Metropolitan airports were snowed in and we were rerouted to Boston. We were able to get a small room on an overnight train. But the room was extremely cold and drafty and Mr. Boehm was concerned about the safety of the precious cargo. He sent me looking for a couple of metal waste baskets while he rounded up all the scrap paper he could find. The conductor was bewildered by this unusual late-hour activity. We then locked the door and all the way to New York Mr. Boehm kept periodic small fires burning in the baskets in order to provide heat for the birds. It almost suffocated us but he got all of the birds to Trenton in good shape."

Musical Moods

Mr. Boehm's preferences for music closely followed his personality moods. In quieter moments he thoroughly enjoyed ballads—the sentimental, storied tunes about life and the life cycle. Among his favorites were "He," "I Believe" and "Honey."

When he was feeling gay and decided to cut loose a bit, he wanted to hear the strength of show tunes and patriotic songs. He loved the music from "Oklahoma" and "Showboat," and he often enjoyed "Battle Hymn of the Republic." (For his wedding music he requested "The Girl That I Marry" or "Be-

Saint
Francis
of
Assissi

cause." His request was denied in favor of the traditional "Ave Maria.") At times he would ask one of his staff to bring in a record player for a day and he would play a tune over and over again. Occasionally he would walk through the studio and sing for all, "belting it out" as his favorite singer, Ethel Merman, would.

Having dinner at his home when he was in the singing mood was quite an experience. He would put on his records of "Oklahoma" and turn the stereo up full blast. This was his idea of good dinner music. On occasion, following dinner, he would decide to record his singing on tape. He never could accept the fact that he could not carry a tune. He would listen to the playback with consternation and, sometimes, anger. I once was with him when he spent a good two hours recording "Old Man River," and each repeat seemed worse than the prior effort.

"...put soul into it..."

But, although he couldn't sing, he insisted he knew how to sing and what good music was all about. Mrs. Boehm has a good voice. He often said she might have had an excellent career in singing popular music. From the time of their marriage he would coach her evenings, showing her how to move, form her notes, "put soul into it," and so on. She became resigned to the fact that when they had guests and he was in a gay mood, she would have to sing his favorite piece, "Paper Doll," which he claimed she performed better than anyone he'd ever heard.

Prized Friends

There are many incidents which may be related concerning Mr. Boehm's deep love and compassion for his animals and birds. As stated, he was more nervous than an expectant father when a calf, foal or rare bird was about to be born.

"...breathed life into the little creature..."

He was a rough individual with the massive hands of a farmer, yet Mrs. Boehm can recall the many times he would splint the legs and wings of birds as small as a hummingbird and perform other merciful tasks to help them. Once he arrived home to find that a pup from his favorite schnauzer had been stillborn, and although considerable time had elapsed, he literally breathed life into the little creature who lived to become one of Mr. Boehm's best dogs.

The animals he kept varied through the years. He even had a pair of otters in one of his ponds and enjoyed their mischievous play, but he had to part with them when, tragically, one of the otters got into the duck pond and ravaged Mr. Boehm's rare duck collection.

Another he was fond of was a young chimpanzee named "Lulu" (see page 46). He kept Lulu in the house for three months, all through the diaper and weaning stage, then sent her to the Taronga Park Zoo in Sydney, Australia, a gift to his friend, Sir Edward Hallstrom.

A most lasting impression was made on me through episodes concerning his fancy fowl—Leghorns, Brahmas, Bantams and Cochins (see page 56). In early 1963 he began to build an important collection. He had not yet obtained the farm and had no room on his home grounds for the fowl so he decided to put them on the second floor above the studio! (At various times in the history of the firm Mr. Boehm had dogs, fowl and fish collections in the studio.) He purchased incubators and began to breed dozens of fine specimens. At one point the number of fowl upstairs numbered approximately 400! During the day we were reminded of their presence above us, especially during the summer months, and the cocks were vociferous early in the morning.

*400
fowl
upstairs!*

Mr. Boehm knew he was not within regulations having the fowl above the studio and he told me not to take the labor investigator upstairs when he made his annual inspection. I almost succeeded in getting by, except that one of the cocks let go with his best barnyard call at the wrong time. We were forced to remove the fowl, but by that time the farm purchase had been negotiated and we had a proper place to keep them.

In the fall of 1964, Mr. Boehm planned to show his best specimens at one important competition held annually in Indianapolis. His preparation for the show revealed the depth of his care. For two months he gave daily attention to the entrants, luxing their feathers, waxing their combs and polishing their toenails. Mrs. Boehm estimated that he devoted an average of two hours each night to this pursuit through this period. He personally drove his fowl to Indianapolis in a station wagon, having two flats in zero weather before arriving. Seven of his ten entries won ribbons.

A Romantic

The old-fashioned, simple things in life appealed to Mr. Boehm, and he often discussed and re-enacted the romantic activities of earlier years. He enjoyed barn dancing and took great pride in his ability to "call" many of the square-dance tunes. When he first started his dairy operation he excitedly told a few of us what fun we would have weekends delivering milk in our neighborhood in white horse-drawn carts, with our daughters handling the door-to-door deliveries in their pretty milk-maid costumes! Somehow we succeeded in discouraging this idea.

Edwin Hart, Mr. Boehm's farm manager, tells of a time in mid-December a few years back when the first snow of the season started to fall. It was a Sunday morning and the phone rang. Mr. Boehm was on the line and said, "Ed, borrow an old sled from one of the neighbors and hook "Good Time Gal" (one of Mr. Boehm's favorite mares) to it. I'll be up in an hour and we'll take your family for a sleigh ride through the fields."

It was no simple task to locate and obtain a sled in an hour, but Ed Hart did. Mr. Boehm arrived, the mare was hooked up, bells were added for the right effect, and off all went. The only trouble was that the plowed ground was soft, the snow was not packed and the runners of the sled were sinking and sticking. It soon was obvious that a good idea was put into action at a wrong time. Good Time Gal was laboring and Mr. Boehm began to worry about her.

Suddenly, after they had gone about a quarter of a mile from the barn, Mr. Boehm said, "Ed, unhook the mare." He then took Good Time Gal in tow and started walking her in. "What should I do with the sled?," said Ed Hart. "Pull it back to the barn," replied Mr. Boehm, "We can't risk having the mare do it."

An Unusual Gift

Mr. Boehm enjoyed buying gifts for children. The giving of young animals gave him the most pleasure, as I was to learn shortly after joining his staff. In his enthusiasm he was often impulsive in his selection.

One day at my home he commented, "I think Laura (my daughter, three years of age at the time) would enjoy having a young nanny goat as a pet." My wife and I nodded feeling the statement was in jest. Not so. The following day Mr. Boehm drove to southern New Jersey and returned in the evening with a beautiful, registered, unweaned nanny.

After three days of uncertainty and apprehension, caused by thoughts of the havoc a growing nanny could bring to a busy, child-overrun suburban community, I reluctantly informed Mr. Boehm that Laura couldn't accept his gift. He was very upset and said, "Why not? A kid couldn't have a better pet! I know you and Nina don't want it, but what about your daughter?"

When I explained the problems of the young children, lack of fencing, and our small property, he still couldn't understand our attitude and said, "Well, then, keep the goat inside. It's a beautiful animal."

"...keep the goat inside."

He finally decided to take the nanny to a friend who had a farm. When leaving he said, "Sometimes I get carried away with my enthusiasm." I always felt he never quite forgave us for not accepting his gift.

Impatience

Edward Marshall Boehm couldn't wait—for anything. Traffic stop signs and lights, television commercials, and the like, bothered him. People later than he for an appointment would find him gone.

The same was true of his work. He wanted immediate results. His aviary and garden building projects were active scenes that seemed disorganized with far too many hands. But there he would be in the midst of all directing equipment and teams of men. Only he knew the results he wanted, and he did obtain them. His pet project theory was, "If you can get a good man to complete a job well in ten days, why not get ten good men and do just as good a job in one day?"

He made his theory work. The beautiful Japanese Garden he built (see page 132), for example, which seemed to have been part of the property for many years, was started and completed in the incredibly short period of thirty-nine days!

A good friend and attorney to Mr. Boehm from the beginning days of the studio, Mr. Harold Coleman, enjoys telling of the many experiences he had with Mr. Boehm's impatience. When he called he expected you to drop everything and answer the phone.

On one occasion Mr. Coleman was in the midst of a very important conference and gave his secretary firm instructions that he was not to be disturbed under any circumstances. Mr. Boehm called and, in spite of the secretary's valiant effort to

hold him off, insisted that he must speak to Mr. Coleman on a matter of extreme importance. Mr. Coleman decided to answer the call. When he picked up the telephone, Mr. Boehm asked, "How can you pay someone $103.00 in cash when you have no singles? What combination of larger bills would you use?" (He never said "hello" or "goodby;" they were time-wasters.)

Having resigned himself to accommodating Mr. Boehm, a lesson learned from prior experience, Mr. Coleman told the bewildered clients in his office to excuse him for a few moments while he made a few computations. He solved the problem and gave Mr. Boehm the answer. As he hung up Mr. Coleman could hear Mr. Boehm say, "See, I knew Harold would come up with the answer right away."

"Moon Gate," formal entrance to the Japanese Gardens. Symbols on the gate are fired into Boehm porcelain plaques. They read, "All those who pass these portals have made the strife worthwhile."

Temper, Temper

The common belief that artists are temperamental was certainly true of Mr. Boehm. He had a fiery temper that none of us wanted to see triggered. All of his friendships and associations had to acclimate to an occasional, torrid argument. He wasn't always right, but he would never apologize. He would let you know indirectly that it might have been his fault by returning to you after ten or fifteen minutes, having, in the interval, conjured up something which he might kid you about to get back on friendly footing.

His temper, plus the usual resistance and encounters met while building an organization, led to his involvement in many hassles, some of them legal. One that carried on for a considerable period involved a champion Cocker Spaniel named "Rickie" (shown above). After having won ribbons in fifty-one competitions, Rickie was suddenly disqualified by a Canadian judge in a Connecticut show. The reason, the judge said, was that Rickie was monorchid. This infuriated Mr. Boehm. "How," he asked, "could he suddenly be monorchid after two years of competition and so many championships?" Mr. Boehm threatened to sue the American Kennel Club. The correspondence in the case, though serious, was sometimes quite humorous. Eventually his anger subsided and the matter was dropped.

Mrs. Boehm relates an incident that occurred during one of the early partnerships. The partner had assigned a young Phi Beta Kappa, recently graduated from one of the finest eastern schools, as business manager and to protect his interests. The young man had a tendency to sit with his feet on his desk and whiled his time reading poetry and writing his diary. His mere presence upset Mr. Boehm and he let the young man know it. One day during an argument, the fledgling manager fired both Mr. and Mrs. Boehm and asked them to leave the building (which at the time was on Stokes Avenue in Trenton). Mrs. Boehm said Mr. Boehm picked him up by the seat of the pants and scruff of the neck, carried him down the steps, and ungracefully threw him out of the building. The young man never returned but he reported an assault charge to the authorities and for a while the matter was serious. The charge eventually was dropped.

I felt Mr. Boehm's wrath on several occasions. Until he got mad, you weren't certain he liked you. He came close to firing me once. Mrs. Boehm and I ran a full-page, national advertisement featuring the "Road Runner." In the copy describing the bird we included its many local names, and just above the head of the sculpture we added the two small, identifying words "beep, beep." We thought this was whimsical and in order. He didn't. He was boiling mad, called the ad a sham, accused me of profaning his art, pointed out that the sculpture was not a toy to be squeezed to make it say "beep, beep," and burned two thousand reprints of the ad which we intended to send to friends. Mrs. Boehm, who was away at the time, delayed her return until the storm passed, but I'm sure the raking she received was also considerable. Waiting on her desk was a copy of the ad with a note in large letters, "We are not in the cartoon or car business."

"... beep beep ..."

The Telephone

A corollary to Mr. Boehm's reluctance to leave his home environment was his great use of the telephone. He called all over the world and sometimes would spend several hours of a day speaking with naturalists, dairy men, farmers, trainers, etc. It was almost impossible to call him in the evening because the line seemed always busy.

But the reverse situation didn't appeal to him. Impulsive and impatient as he was, he would become perturbed if he wanted to speak with you or show you something and you were occupied with a telephone conversation. He felt Mrs. Boehm and I spent too much time on the telephone! At times he would burst into the office and say to Mrs. Boehm or me, "Hang up the phone, quick, I have something to show you." To avoid embarrassment we would cover the phone and try to explain that the party on the end of the line was important and was calling about business. This didn't stop him. His usual retort was, "Well turn him off, this is much more important." Generally he wanted our attention to tell us of a new milk record one of his cows made, or a new time mark made by one of his pacers, or to show us, through sketches, how a perfect udder or tailset should look.

Doodles

Treasured byproducts of his telephone activity were the beautiful drawings and doodles he would create while engaged. He had to have a pencil and pad handy before he would make a call. The small vignettes throughout the book are from his renderings. The montages of sketches also were "telephone-created."

The Cuckoo Clock

One October day Mr. Boehm and I planned to attend a professional football game in Philadelphia. He had secured front-row tickets and although I was moving to another home that same day, he wouldn't let me refuse his invitation.

He arrived at our home at about 11 a.m. Nina, my wife, was busily unpacking cartons. Just as Mr. Boehm and I were set to leave, she asked if she should throw out an inexpensive cuckoo clock which had been severely damaged in moving. Mr. Boehm asked to see the clock. When I handed it to him I said, "Let her throw it away, it can't be fixed." That was the wrong thing to say. It stirred his interest and the challenge was joined. "I can fix it; it will only take a few minutes," he said.

"I can fix it ..."

The challenge was much greater than he anticipated, but he refused to leave until the clock was repaired. Game time came and passed, and so did most of the day. About six hours and many angry expressions later, the clock was working perfectly again, and he was pleased. He had no regrets at all about having missed the football contest.

Forced Interests

People Edward Boehm was fond of had to learn to love animals. He insisted on it. To involve them so they were forced to give attention and time, he had a practice of convincing them to buy an animal in partnership with him. Not all of these arrangements worked to the benefit of the partners. The monorchid Cocker Spaniel, "Rickie," discussed in the vignette "Temper, Temper," was partly owned by the unfortunate Mr. Harold Coleman, who, as Mr. Boehm's attorney, ironically wound up also being burdened with all the work while Mr. Boehm was contemplating litigating the case.

Mr. Coleman revealed how he got involved. Mr. Boehm would often say to him, "Harold, what you need is ownership of a real good animal so I can get you interested." When Rickie came along, in the course of a conversation Mr. Boehm mentioned that he finally had an animal Harold should partly own. To appease him, Harold said okay, thinking that there would be so little involved anyway. Later when he received the bill he learned that he had bought part ownership in a dog to the tune of $750!

Friends similarly involved included his physician Dr. Bernard J. Ronis; our accountant, Mr. Frank Suplee; Mr. Oliver H. Delchamps, Mr. Morris Gastwirth and others we probably don't even know about.

At times, even when he gave an animal as a gift, he imposed a slight financial burden so you might appreciate it more. Miss Barbara Hanley of C. D. Peacock, one of the first buyers of Mr. Boehm's art and a long-time close friend, once received a gift of a schnauzer from Mr. Boehm. After telling him it would be difficult to keep a dog where she lived, he sent it anyway and he shipped it collect!

". . . he shipped it collect!"

The Judge

Mr. Boehm considered worthwhile his service as a judge for the Miss America Pageant and the Junior Miss Pageant. He particularly enjoyed the latter because the girls were younger.

After his third term with the Miss America Pageant he decided not to serve again. The girls he selected did not win and he became discouraged with the selection process. He believed that more importance should be given to shape, that finalists should be selected primarily on their points of conformation just as one would select a top dog, horse or cow in animal competitions.

Furthermore, he said the panel of judges always was weighted heavily with theatrical personalities, so the tendency was to lean toward the girls with theatrical abilities. He felt natural beauty and basic talents were more important and better typified the all-American girl.

" . . . all the better . . ."

His selections in the three years were two girls from Wisconsin and one from Michigan. As he said in a four-page critique sent to the Pageant committee, "Miss America should have natural beauty and near-perfect conformation. If she knows how to ride a horse, milk a cow, trim out a dog, all the better. . . ."

Personnel

In the first few years of my association with the firm it was not easy working with personnel while under the scrutiny of Mr. Boehm. He wanted to be aware of every phase of the operation. Furthermore, he maintained he could tell the potential of a person by the look of their eyes, the pace and style of their movements, appearance, etc.

To my chagrin, most of the time he was right. I eventually learned to appreciate his opinions and I gained by doing so, but never fully appreciated his approach. Typical comments would be, "Don't tell me you hired that person. Can't you see he'll never make it! Boy, you have a lot to learn."

"Boy, you have a lot to learn . . ."

But, as I've indicated, he wasn't always right. A few people that I argued strongly for turned out to be excellent additions to our staff. Only recently Mrs. Boehm told me of the great problem she faced when she hired me. First of all, Mr. Boehm had already had one unsatisfactory experience with an Ivy League graduate. Secondly, he became suspect when he learned I was an ex-athlete with stenographic skills. Thirdly, he was reluctant to hire a person in the executive capacity intended.

I know now that I owe Mrs. Boehm a debt of gratitude for her fortitude and faith. She said that on an average of once

a week during my first six months of employment he would pop his head into her office as he passed by and remark, "When are you going to get rid of that kid."

"Throwing The Bull"

In May of 1968 we held a two-day conference in Trenton attended by executives of the fine stores and galleries which represent Boehm porcelains. The purpose of this and other conferences is for the establishment of closer relationships, introduction of new collections and an interchange of marketing policies and ideas. Approximately sixty guests were present (see above).

An important part of the itinerary, as requested by Mr. Boehm, was a dinner at Duncravin Farm in the horse barn. This beautiful, Early American building has a central corridor through its length. All were asked to arrive dressed "Dogpatch" style, small tables with checkered, gingham table cloths were placed about, cocktails were offered from stalls, hors d'oeuvres and dinner were served from an authentic covered wagon, a professional square dance group was on hand to demonstrate

The Boehm Conference, May 9, 1969. Executives of galleries and stores attended a two-day symposium at the Boehm home and gardens. The guests are viewing the 1969 porcelain collection.

and teach barn dances, and Mr. Boehm suggested that all should have at least one glass of raw milk from his best Holstein cows.

Midway through the evening Mr. Boehm decided to show the animals he was most proud of. He suddenly appeared at the entrance to the barn with "King's Arctic Rose" (see page 51) in hand, asked that the music be stopped, had the tables moved to the walls and started walking Rose through. He was as proud as a doting father and showed the intense affection he held for his animals. He addressed our guests on the fine points of Rose telling of her great milk production records, lineage and honors. When he finished speaking about her he asked if there were any questions, hoping someone might ask about udder conformation, tail-set, etc. Finally, one of our guests, Mr. Mark Scearce of Wakefield-Scearce Galleries, asked, "How much does she weigh, Ed?" Mr. Boehm replied, pointedly, "Damn it, Mark, when you take a beautiful girl on a date, do you ask her how much she weighs?"

". . . do you ask her how much she weighs?"

Moving a one-ton animal like Rose through the barn required considerable time, but Mr. Boehm had just begun. He returned with Rose's fifteen-year old mother, "Canary" (see page 51) and then again with a young bull, "Royal Results," for whom he had great hopes. Eventually our guests became a bit restless. Conversation picked up by the time the young bull arrived. Mr. Boehm could see that he was losing some attentions and this irritated him. He shouted so all could hear, "Will you stop throwing the bull for a minute and take a look at a real bull!" (Royal Results later won his first competition, First Prize, Yearling Bull, New Jersey Black and White, August 19, 1969.)

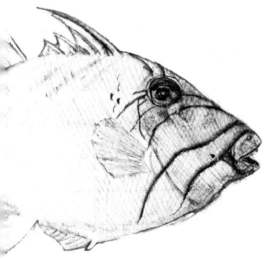

The Fish Collection

Mr. Boehm's tropical fish collection was exceptional. He acquired many of the most beautiful species in the world and kept them in elaborate, built-in tanks in the basement of his home. The tank environs were carefully planned with different types and colors of coral and the correct plants.

His collection was unusual in that it was primarily of salt-water fish. He said that the most beautiful in color and ornamentation were salt-water tropicals. The problems of keeping these specimens are well beyond the comparatively simple task of keeping fresh-water varieties. Temperature and salinity factors were critical and had to be accurate and constant.

Edwin Hart recently told Mrs. Boehm that one day while attending to his duties at the farm he received a telephone call from Mr. Boehm. He was told that from then on he was responsible for periodically taking a tanker truck down to the New Jersey sea coast to collect natural sea water for the fish. For that moment, however, he told Ed to take his pickup truck down to the shore, rent a small row boat and fetch several barrels to hold them over. And, said Mr. Boehm, "Be sure you go out at least a couple of hundred yards and only collect when the tide is coming in. I want good fresh sea water!"

". . . good fresh sea water!"

What Mr. Boehm didn't know, as he wasn't in a mood that day for comments or questions, was that Ed Hart can't swim and wanted no part of the Atlantic Ocean. But, valor prevailed and the mission was completed. Ed Hart said, "Mr. Boehm was like that. He had a way of getting you to do things you never thought you'd do."

Culinary Largess

Eating was spontaneous and accidental for Edward Boehm. He ate when he was hungry, not when he was supposed to. Mrs. Boehm learned early in her marriage not to try to hold him to a particular time for dinner, and not to expect him necessarily to eat what had been prepared. If he became involved in a project, he would not come in for dinner at all, even though he might have invited guests to join him.

He loved to eat out of the refrigerator and he ate all of the wrong foods, heavy salads, a couple of quarts of milk a day, ice cream and other sweets and lots of coffee. He cared not at all for vegetables and fruit. Fancy foods did not appeal to him.

At times he would have a desire to cook. One day late in 1968 he came into the offices grumbling about how boring his food had been lately. He was going to change that. As he often would do, he sent one of his artisans who knew him best (either Elaine Swain or Gertrude Davis, two of his first staff supervisors) to shop for foods he liked and hadn't had in a long time, including live snails. Later in the day he told me to call my wife and tell her to meet me at his house for dinner. He was going to prepare escargot and gumbo for us! He also was going to make sweet potato pie and corn bread, two of his favorites.

". . . live snails."

He must have been in the kitchen for two hours, then sat down to watch us eat what he had prepared. Each course was good, but not as good as he expected us to tell him it was. Later Mrs. Boehm whispered to me, "It can't have been too tasty. He accidentally ground up half of a rubber spatula in the gumbo!"

Occasionally he would accept a dinner invitation. A hostess soon learned that this could be a discouraging experience, but never dull. There were times when he would arrive and announce that he wanted no dinner, only coffee, that "people eat too much anyway." It was obvious he had raided his refrigerator before coming. If he decided to eat and the hostess asked him if he were enjoying it, he would give one of two honest answers, "not so good" or "not bad."

An experience my family and I cherish occurred just three evenings before Mr. Boehm's transition. Mrs. Boehm was away and we invited him to dinner. Nina worked all day preparing gumbo as he liked it and was in the process of cooking a roast when he arrived. In he came carrying a gallon of gumbo under one arm and a gallon of raw oysters under the other. A friend had sent them from Mobile and they arrived that day.

He walked into the kitchen and said, "Get rid of that stuff, throw it out. We're going to eat some real gumbo and I'm going to teach you how to cook oysters." Well, my wife had become conditioned to him and learned not to become upset nor to resist in any way. The stove was cleared and the lessons began. For my part, I spent a good share of the evening driving about town looking for corn meal, lard and all the special items he had to have.

"I never eat my own cooking."

He made Oysters Rockefeller, oyster stew and deep-fried oysters. We had mounds of oysters, enough for at least a dozen adults. The crowning stroke was when we finally sat down for dinner. He pushed his plate away and blandly announced, "I never eat my own cooking."

From Confusion—Beauty

The most frustrating time of the year for Mr. Boehm's key artisans was early spring. This was when the prototypes of new sculptures had to be completed for May introductions. Apart from the normal pressures of coordinating efforts and ironing out design and structural details, Mr. Boehm was not entirely cooperative in his work routine and attention. The new models always conflicted with his spring gardening programs. Also, he enjoyed working under pressure and would become motivated and activated just before deadlines. This, of course, forced an equal pressure on his artisans.

Maurice Eyeington, Mr. Boehm's assistant sculptor, often had to follow through with eleventh-hour, major changes in the sculptures, and this resulted in changes down the line from the moldmakers through the shipping department. The pressure was particularly heavy on Frank Surro and Bill Kazmar, key artisans involved in the ending phases of the process, the painting and final touches.

But although each spring there were the normal grumblings and a great deal of confusion, each person involved later would admit, with pleasure and pride, that the results were right and beautiful.

The Frustrated Spectator

Mr. Boehm's propensity for athletics has been documented in foregoing portions of this work. It also has been reported that his ability while participating in some of the various sports not always was commensurate with his enthusiasm. But he kept trying, nevertheless.

His credo, revealing a remarkable will to win, may be found in an expression he used on more than one occasion: "Show me a happy loser and I'll show you an idiot."

I have related that he participated, semi-professionally, in football and boxing as a young man. His ventures into other sports also have been touched upon. But football, both on the collegiate and professional levels, remained an abiding passion and was capable of drawing him from home as perhaps few other interests, beside his beloved birds and animals, could.

The closing weeks of his life were brightened with a trip south to the Senior Bowl football game in Mobile, Alabama, and the Super Bowl championship between the New York Jets and the Baltimore Colts in Miami.

Keyed up as always for these games, the fact that late-arriving celebrities at the Super Bowl were detracting from the action on the playing field was just too much for him to bear. As the tardy celebrities struggled through to seats and some spectators craned necks to see them, all the while ignoring the

Late arrivals.

143

growing drama as the Jets built toward their upset victory, Mr. Boehm, in a typically resounding comment, shouted: "Hell, did we come here to watch the celebrities or see a football game? Sit down!"

Over the din, devoted football fans in the section of the stadium around him turned toward Mr. Boehm and obviously welcomed the scolding, searing comment. From that point on concentration properly was focused away from the celebrities to the action on the field below.

A Love Of Teaching

Edward Boehm gave a good part of his time to teaching those of us around him. He loved to give instruction. The key artisans and staff members who worked closely with him constantly had the benefit of his counsel.

One member of our staff, Dominick Angelini, presently our head supervisor, was the recipient of a lot of attention. With Mr. Boehm's instructions he built the aviary and farm structures, helped plan and plant the beautiful gardens, learned the art of topiary, and renovated the studio. Dom was in charge of every architectural and construction project over a period of twelve years and Mr. Boehm involved him in some facets of the porcelain process as well.

Dom fondly recalls the circumstances surrounding the time Mr. Boehm insisted that he learn the identities of all birds in the aviaries. On occasion rare specimens would escape through a door inadvertently left open or a hole in the wire netting. Mr. Boehm's talking Cockatoo once left and was gone for three days. Others to escape were a Rifle Bird (relative of the Birds of Paradise), a White-booted Racquet-tailed Hummingbird, and a Golden-crowned Crane. All eventually were recaptured.

When the large, four-foot-tall Crane escaped, Mr. Boehm sent Dom and a few helpers in search, beating through the bushes along the Delaware. It was no easy task to catch a bird of this size and mobility. A good part of the day passed before the team was finally successful. Dom proudly returned to Mr. Boehm with a large box containing the bird. On opening the box Mr. Boehm was startled to see a large, domestic Heron, not the Golden-crowned Crane of Africa. That was when he ordered Dom to learn the characteristics and identifications of all birds in the aviaries!

"...domestic Heron..."

144

For A Friend

In a prior sub-section I referred to Mr. Boehm's friends and the solid, deep relationships he would weld. He repeatedly welcomed them to call on him at any time for assistance or advice. His care and manner were brotherly. He enjoyed his friends to the extent that he constantly boosted them to others and "went to bat" for them in all kinds of situations.

Following is a letter written by Mr. Boehm for Mr. Del Cameron, advisor, trainer and driver for Mr. Boehm's harness horses. It is an urgent and eloquent plea for publicity in behalf of a dear friend. (See following page.)

Mrs. Boehm, driver and trainer Del Cameron, and groom "Uta" with "Miss Step N." at Brandywine Raceway, June 24, 1967. One of Mr. Boehm's favorites, Miss Step N. won her race in 2:04:1.

The Spirit Of Christmas

The day before Christmas of each year the spirit of the Holiday Season completely permeated Mr. Boehm. Prior to this he seemed unaware of it. The result usually was a frantic trip to New York City in an effort to purchase his gifts.

On each occasion a friend or associate was asked to go along. To be in New York City the day before Christmas was enervating; to do so with Mr. Boehm was a nerve-rending experience. Enroute he would decide on all gifts. On arrival the whirlwind set into motion up and down Fifth Avenue and around the city.

Edward Marshall Boehm, Inc.

PORCELAIN OBJECTS OF ART

February 15, 1968

Mr. Eugene F. Fairbanks, Editor
Hoof Beats Magazine
750 Michigan Avenue
Columbus, Ohio 43215

Dear Mr. Fairbanks:

I am writing to inquire if I might arouse your interest in doing an article on a
man, Del Cameron, who in my estimation and that of many others, because of his
quiet, unassuming nature, has perhaps been overlooked and consequently, been devoid
of the publicity his know-how and ability so well deserve.

I have had personal contact over the last few years with both Del and his family, and
I consider them one of American's real grass roots of the racing game. In daily
personal associations with him, his warmth and inner integrity leave nothing to be
desired. His outlook on life, his treatment of animals, his dealings with men warm
the cockles of your heart, because his servitude toward both is most admirable. I
have, on many occasions, observed him to return at midnight on the premise that his
mind carried doubts as to the well-being of a particular horse. When the occasion
has presented itself, I have been a silent eavesdropper, and have heard many of the
brighter lights ask his opinion as to how to "hang a horse". His knowledge is always
given cheerfully and freely, and never in a supercilious manner.

His owners are always treated in the same unassuming manner - directly and truth-
fully, without any intent of false hopes.

It is the opinion of many (and I am sure you personally share this opinion) that he
is one of the great "complete horsemen" of this era; i.e., I use the word horseman
because I think that title far better describes and defines his total, rather than
categorical, ability.

I feel quite sure, with a little prodding, one could derive a world of know-how from
"the quiet one". One cannot disregard the irrefutable fact that this man has taken
three Hambletonians with non-favorites; and between you and me, this unobtrusive man
has an ace up his sleeve, and has a "dark horse" under wraps, so that when the sun
sets on the Hambletonian this year, he may again have some people pulling their hair.

And I do think that you will agree, again, that his uncommon loyalty has perhaps kept
him from obtaining the meteorical heights which his abilities warrant.

I trust that some time in the near future our paths will cross and I will have the
pleasure of meeting you. I should enjoy hearing from you relative to the above.

Sincerely yours,

Edward Marshall Boehm

EMB:mac

One excursion I was on coincided with a snowstorm, and it was a trip when the gift emphasis was on bigness. Cabs were not only scarce but wouldn't have stopped for us anyway. We wound up walking twenty-five blocks in the snow. He carried a five-foot stuffed giraffe over one shoulder and a set of golf clubs on the other; and I was equally laden. He vowed never to repeat the experience, but each year he would do the same. He simply couldn't get excited about Christmas until the day before.

"... a five-foot stuffed giraffe ..."

This all-encompassing spirit came in many forms. A former staff member told me of the time he received a call on Christmas Eve and heard, "I'll pick you up in ten minutes. We're going to fill the station wagon with groceries and drop them off to a couple of families across the river who really need it. Also, call the fuel company and tell them to send a few tons of coal so they will have heat in the house."

Another time I was called and Mr. Boehm said, "I'm pruning about a hundred fowl from the flock at the farm and am having them dressed. How about taking them into town and handing them out to people who really could use them?" I suggested it might be better to arrange for their distribution through one of the welfare agencies rather than risk disorder which could result through a "handing-out." I won my point but not before I was chastised by him for my lack of the spirit of Christmas. I had unintentionally removed the spontaneity and pleasure from his gesture.

One of the warmest experiences that can be told about Mr. Boehm and Christmas occurred in 1964 when he decided to be Santa Claus for two small children at our home—our daughter and the daughter of Mr. and Mrs. John Maddock, long-time family friends of the Boehms.

Mr. Boehm approached the evening full of excitement. Authenticity and perfection were the order. The suit, boots and makeup had to be just right and resulted in a costume which was stifling from its thickness and weight. Mrs. Boehm and we, the parents, were carefully coached in our roles.

"... carefully coached ..."

About 10 p.m. there was a clanging of cow bells and we all ran dutifully to the large front window. Passing by several times at a frisky gait was a reindeer head which Mr. Boehm had borrowed. He crouched low so only the bobbing head could be seen. The bells were hung on his belt for clatter. Finally the door burst open and in came Santa Claus, minus the deer head and bells which had been discarded, bellowing a hearty "ho, ho, ho."

*Alba
Madonna*

The dramatic noisy entrance coupled with Mr. Boehm's deep, loud voice, unfortunately frightened one of the children (Thank goodness it wasn't ours!). The scene was raucous. The child cried hysterically insisting that Santa should immediately go back to the North Pole and never return. Even removing Santa to another room didn't help, and the parents were powerless. The result was that Santa had to leave the house, but not before slumping in a chair for a momentary rest. Later Mr. Boehm told us that he had almost passed out from the heat and exertion of the disappointing experience. To my knowledge the child distrusted Santa Claus for several seasons thereafter.

"There Is My Tabernacle"

Edward Boehm's religion was not communal and on Sunday. Yet he expressed a constant awareness of The Divine Being. His feelings of religion were solitary. His God was seen in the beauty and orderliness of nature and her creatures.

Mrs. Boehm relates a story about a February early morning Sunday breakfast at home. As she was preparing for church the subject of discussion was religion and his failure to attend mass. The conversation became deep and probing. Mr. Boehm was having difficulty defining his feelings and he was becoming frustrated. Suddenly a brilliant male Cardinal flew to a snow-laden branch of the big spruce adjacent to the window. With pause and a relaxing expression Mr. Boehm asked Mrs. Boehm to turn to the window and said, "There is my tabernacle, and there is my religion."

Edward Marshall Boehm's
Gardens AND Aviaries . . .

Edward Marshall Boehm's gardens and aviaries brought him as much attention from aviculturists and botanists as his sculptures did from patrons and students of his art. Each garden and aviary was designed by him and the latter incorporated innovations in bird care that attracted zoo directors, naturalists and ornithologists from all over the world.

Scientific journals and publications such as the internationally-subscribed "Avicultural Magazine" of England looked forward to articles about Mr. Boehm's collection and work and willingly gave prime space and attention to each one submitted.

Apart from the beauties and rarities of his collection, Mr. Boehm's skill with life, his sensitivity to it, extraordinary communication with it, is evident through his work with live birds. In so short a period of time he brought together perhaps the greatest collection of insectivorous birds ever assembled; and he housed them in such tranquil, natural surroundings that more than fifty of these rare species bred successfully, many for the first time in captivity, while under his care.

It might not be an exaggeration to say that Mr. Boehm know more about insectivorous birds of the world than any ornithologist or aviculturist before him. He lived with them for years, studied them daily, understood them in depth, was happy when new young were born and fared well, sorrowed when others were lost, and looked at all through the eyes both of the artist and scientist that he was.

The importance of this phase of Edward Boehm's work, like his art, will continue to grow with the passage of time. In ornithology today, with few exceptions, the era of the large private collection is a thing of the past. Birds of the world have been decimated in the last few decades and, to protect the remaining species, most countries are imposing embargos severely limiting further exportations. Mr. Boehm was able to acquire his rarities only because his excellent grounds and accommodations earned him zoological status and attendant privileges.

The most meaningful tributes to Mr. Boehm for his contributions to aviculture come from world-respected colleagues and friends who devote their lives to the study and welfare of live birds of the world. An excellent article entitled "Gardens of Inspiration" appeared in the April 1963 issue of "Zoonooz," monthly publication of the San Diego Zoo. The author, Mr. Kenton C. Lint, Curator of Birds at the Zoo,

Previous page shows Mr. Boehm in "Indian Gardens" aviary throwing meal worms to its inhabitants.

had visited with Mr. Boehm to accept from him a gift of thirty-six species. The first two paragraphs of Mr. Lint's article embody some of his impressions:

"A visit to one of the finest private collections of insectivorous birds in the world today is well worth sharing with all of our readers. Its owner, Edward Marshall Boehm, realized early in his career that he would need live models if he were to capture the true beauty of birds at rest and in flight. The first aviary was designed and constructed eight years ago. Immediately he began to collect the needed live models from many parts of the world, especially birds from Africa, Australia, India, New Guinea, Eurasia and North and South America.

"The success and fame of the Boehm bird sculptures demanded new live models and larger housing facilities for the increasing number of birds. Presently the enclosures on the estate at Washington Crossing are of impressive proportions. All are landscaped with luxuriant foliage. Various decorative effects are achieved with English Ivy, Bird's-nest Fern, Ficus, Calla, bamboo, azaleas, philodendrons, begonias, fuchsias, freesia, pelargoniums, spireas, New Zealand Ginger, and impatiens. Networks of circulating miniature brooks wind artistically among the plantings, cascading over tiny waterfalls, around rock formations, and forming tiny pools."

". . . luxuriant foliage."

Doctor Jean Delacour of Cleres, France, in writing about the aviaries, described them as "truly magnificent aviaries of great size, beautifully landscaped." He said of Mr. Boehm, "Ed Boehm, being keen, clever and active beyond belief, managed to obtain within a few years the many rare species he wanted from all parts of the world;" and of the bird collection, "Rare species, seldom if ever seen alive before, figured in his collection and many reared young at Trenton for the first time in captivity."

"Rare species . . ."

One of Mr. Boehm's closest colleagues, a man who knew him and his work thoroughly, is Mr. Charles Everitt, an English-born aviculturist who joined Mr. Boehm's staff late in 1959 as curator of the aviaries and, today, continues in charge.

Over the years Mr. Everitt has cataloged the collection and breedings and has recorded voluminous notes on the important scientific observations of the various species. His articles have appeared in several scientific journals, and at present he is compiling in book form the total experience of Mr. Boehm's avicultural work. Following are a few excerpts from his notes entitled "Memories of Edward Marshall Boehm."

"Basically he was a lover of nature in all its forms, be it animal, vegetable, or mineral. Coupled with this adoration was his skill with his hands in sculpting the creatures he loved. The words 'can not be done' were anathema to him. The purpose of the aviaries was not just to satisfy his craving to be near to nature, but to provide him with living models for his porcelain creations, and to prove to the world that his contention, that correct feeding in the right environment would result in the propagation of the species, was substantiated.

"He studied assiduously to ascertain what each species lived on in its country of origin, their mating and nesting habits, and then proceeded to meet these requirements as far as humanly possible. 'Paradise Flycatchers' being fed on the wing with mealworms, crickets and moths every two hours for three to four days after arrival, and then gradually being drawn down to the feeding dishes. Hollowed out sweet potatoes being filled with mealworms and 'planted' in the floor of the flight for newly-arrived Hoopoes. These are but two of the simpler schemes he devised to 'meat-off' rare acquisitions. It would take volumes to go into all the details of the diets he formulated and the many, many other ways in which he contributed to the care and welfare of his beloved winged creatures. With the eyes of a hawk he could see at a flash a bird that was off colour and needed hospitalization.

". . . It (aviaries) was never operated as a commercial enterprise, all birds surplus to his needs being donated to zoological gardens throughout the United States, and some even going to Paris. His passing leaves a wide gap in the field of aviculture. It was not a field to Edward Marshall Boehm, but a science, and, as such, a challenge to be met.

"Reticent by nature, at times so intense that his manner simulated boredom when in company, you could be sure that, in every waking moment, he was just thinking of some way in which he could get even closer to nature."

Our final source must be quoted. Sir Edward Hallstrom of Sydney, Australia, Director of the Taronga Park Zoo, was a dear friend of Mr. Boehm and one of the men Mr. Boehm most respected for his work in the conservation and perpetuation of all species of life. Sir Edward served as protector to the Birds of Paradise of New Guinea and controlled their limited distribution to zoological societies around the world.

". . . sweet potatoes . . ."

". . . even closer to nature."

152

It was he who arranged for Mr. Boehm to receive sixteen magnificent pairs of these fabled birds. He was thrilled when Mr. Boehm succeeded in breeding three species for the first time in captivity. In a letter to Mrs. Boehm, Sir Edward wrote:

"Ed was such a wonderful fellow it is so hard for a layman not used to writing to put his pen to paper and write just a few words that tell a great story of a great man. I regard him as just that. I have seen quite a lot of his work and I have imagined being left alone in a room with some of his fascinating thoughts portrayed in the materials used by him; I found it so hard to say the things I would like to say. Ed Boehm the man, scientist, ornithologist, aviculturist, ceramist almost defies description. God bless his soul."

To allow insight into the depth of feeling and involvement of Mr. Boehm with his live birds, in the following pages are presented two articles written by him. The first appeared in the June 1962 issue of "Frontiers," a magazine of natural history published by The Academy of Natural Sciences of Philadelphia. Its title is "Velvet Birds In Our Gardens." The second, "Successful Breedings At The Edward Marshall Boehm Aviaries In 1966," was published in the July-August 1967 issue of "The Avicultural Magazine," published by The Avicultural Society.

Velvet Birds in Our Gardens

A few months ago, Sir Edward Hallstrom, of Sydney, Australia and Nondugl, West Highlands, New Guinea, noted philanthropist, zoo director, aviculturist and possessor of probably the world's largest collection of birds of paradise and psittacine birds, kindly presented to me six true pairs of birds of paradise. These and others previously acquired, are now housed in enclosed, heated gardens in our Washington Crossing aviaries.

Seven species of birds of paradise are represented in the gardens: the twelve-wired bird of paradise, Seleucides melanoleucus; lesser birds of paradise, Paradisia minor; red-plumed bird of paradise or count raggiana, Paradisia raggiana; blue bird of paradise, Paradisornis rudolphi; princess stephanie, Astrarchia stephaniae; original rifle bird or velvet bird, Ptiloris paradiseus; and the magnificent bird of paradise, Diphyllodes magnifica.

In brief, the classification of these birds is as follows: the family name is Paradiseidae. The Paradiseidae, in turn, contains 13 genera and 43 species.

"...a single region of the world..."

Birds of paradise are restricted to a single region of the world, the Papuan (New Guinea and neighboring islands), with the exception of three species found down the East Coast of Australia. Our collection includes a pair of one of these Australian species, the original rifle bird of Northern New South Wales and Southern Queensland.

I am going to speak specifically on the rifle bird, Ptiloris paradiseus, and my observations on it in captivity. Our pair is housed in a 20′ x 40′ x 16′ enclosed garden, landscaped with white pine, rhododendron, azalea, ilex and hydrangea. We have observed that the birds particularly delight in removing the buds of rhododendron, more, I think, for amusement than nourishment, although I think they eat a small percentage of the buds.

A huge 60′ oak grows through the top of the aviary. Both male and female continuously probe the deep, serrated bark, evidently in quest of insects. They also probe the plastic which covers their enclosure for the winter months. They hang by the hour, upside down, sideways, and what-have-you, puncturing the plastic with their long bills, so that the covering has to be replaced every few weeks.

They also drive everyone crazy by manipulating the alarm thermostat, which rings a loud bell if the temperature should drop below a set point. You can well imagine this bell ringing every twenty or thirty minutes and everyone dashing to the heating unit—only to discover that Mr. Ptiloris paradiseus is sitting calmly on top of the unit heater, reaching down with his ever-so-sensitive bill, quietly maneuvering the temperature control lever back and forth.

"...drove everyone crazy..."

In order to push the lever, Mr. Ptiloris paradiseus has to go through a ¼″ grid guard before reaching the control. This probing technique seems to go on at all levels. There remains hardly a leaf that is not flipped over with great agility. The birds seem as adept at terrestrial maneuvering as at arboreal. Their relatively short tibia is terminated by strong, powerful toes and talons, almost hawk-like in grasp and strength, strong enough to pierce one's finger.

Our rifle birds are gourmands. They consume a formula of chopped bananas, ground apples, ground oranges, ground grapes, ground carrots; plus an insectivorous mix of liver meal, fish meal, bone meal, middlings, whole-wheat flour, hard-boiled eggs; to which are added toasted bread crumbs and a carotinoid oil. The mixture is rolled into small, berry-like balls, because they feed by picking up objects by the tips of their mandibles, tossing them into the air with a quick, agile movement and catching them in the backs of their mouths.

In addition to the above, they are fed fresh-ground beef hearts twice a day. Also, each receives twenty-five to thirty mealworms twice a day, plus a half dozen crickets (raised here at the aviaries), and as a tidbit, twice a week, a small hairless white mouse.

"...ground beef hearts twice a day."

The photographs which accompany this article show the male bird in immature plumage. It is very similar to the hen's, except for almost indiscernible differences; such as the barring being a little closer in pattern and the width of the barring itself. When the male reaches mature plumage (between five and six years of age) he carries the following pattern and colors:

The bill is black, and the frontal feathers which grow on the nostril lid are velvety black. The feathers of the top and back of the head are small and scale-like, closely rucked and shining with a metallic sheen, from blue-green to a most brilliant emerald. The sides of the head show a bronzy tinge. The back rump and upper tail coverts are velvety black, with a wash of brown. The feathers of the upper back are longer, forming somewhat of a cape. The wing feathers are a blackish-brown, with the secondaries blacker, tinged with purple; the tail feathers are coal black, with the exception of the central pair, which are a beautiful, shining metallic blue-green.

Underneath the chin, the feathers are very small and velvety black, but the throat and upper breast feathers show an elongated triangle of long, narrow, scale-like feathers, scintillating with the iridescence of blue-green. The lower angles extend a little, forming what is known as the breast shield; the sides of the breast and the broad band across the lower breast are deep, velvety black. Succeeding this band, the feathers broaden and show an edging of silvery green which grows more extensive, concealing entirely the velvet black bases. Lower, the feathers also lengthen, but remain broad and dense. The under-color of the wings and tail is black. The legs are black; the eyes, dark brown.

The female has the bill more brownish, with a basal paleness. The marginal color of the breast and side plumes is a deep, almost chocolate brown, while the overall color of the back and tail is an olivy-brown.

I don't think I have ever possessed birds having greater intelligence. They seem much cleverer than any other form of paradise bird with which I have been associated, and they are not nearly so laconic as the other species of Paradiseidae.

Perhaps their high place on the ladder of avifaunal intelligence can best be observed through the elaborate dancing rituals of the males and, on rare occasions, the females. It has been observed that there is a great degree of variance in the repertoire of individual males and also that the degree of intensity varies with each male.

To better describe this most interesting phase of their lives, the dance ritual, I have prepared a series of photographs sequelled, as nearly as possible, from the beginning to the end of display. I do not wish to convey the thought that this

". . . from blue-green to a most brilliant emerald."

is a set pattern or sequence, as it can and does assume many manifestations. One likes to think of it as a ballet—and with that thought in mind, let me set the stage and give you the lighting.

The time—a quiet spring morn—Old Sol, wakening from his bed of horizons, finds that his blanket of clouds has silently fallen from his form—his predicament sends a pink glow of embarrassment to the very portals of Heaven itself. From the quiet of this panorama bursts the rifle bird to a loftier perch, there better to view the encounters to come. The sound of his flight has been likened to the rustle of satin.

The rifle bird now turns to his toiletry—that of putting his plumage in order, like a dancer giving his costume one final check before facing the footlights—then on to his repertoire. (see pages 158, 159).

The dance stage is used over and over again and seems always to be an object of surface area, rather than a mere branch or perch.

It is truly a remarkable performance to witness "live." I have observed that on occasion the female becomes bored with the whole procedure and ignores the male entirely. After a period of futile efforts to attract her, the male will fly to a branch nearby or even cling to the wire of the adjoining aviary and proceed to dance for any bird that is flying within his scope of vision. I once saw him emote for a hummingbird that happened to be feeding in suspended flight in front of him. The rifle bird, at this point, seemed to be like a small boy who has just learned to balance a broom and wishes to show his accomplishment to just anyone.

Edward Marshall Boehm

"Frontiers"

ONE—The male "Rifle Bird" casually stretches his wings, first right, then left.

TWO—Stretching himself to his full height he peals out with a loud raucous call of "yaas, yaas."

Dance of the Rifle Bird c

FIVE—She now increases her speed of flight, flying faster and faster, coming ever closer with fewer intervals of rest. The tempo of his dance picks up. His pirouetting increases. Whirling and wheeling he extends his wings to the fullest in an umbrellic arc.

SIX—Now tension has reached its peak. He begins to snap his head from side to side with mandibles open to their fullest, showing the bright apple green of their interior to her.

THREE—Then suddenly he seems to click into position and becomes an animated toy, as it were. It is here that one feels his tension.

FOUR—He now becomes as one drugged by the passion of his feelings, completely unconscious of everything but his love-to-be. The female Rifle Bird begins to fly back and forth in the area of his vision apparently oblivious to his presence. He begins to bow and scrape turning always to face her line of flight.

ustralia

EIGHT—The climax is reached when she, no longer able to resist the rapture, flies to the edge of the stage where he enfolds her within his wings.

SEVEN—The snapping of his head at this point becomes so malevolent that the "cracking" of the bones of the neck is audible, as is the impact of the head itself against the bow of the wings—and all the while he calls loudly, clearly, "yaas, yaas, yaas."

Successful Breedings at
The Edward Marshall Boehm Aviaries in 1966

I am pleased to relate some of the interesting breedings we have accomplished at the Edward Marshall Boehm Aviaries in 1966. First, I will mention, collectively, breedings which I think have not been accomplished heretofore, and I use the work "think" advisedly, because I have no definite way of confirming this.

Came first the breeding of the Princess Stephanie's Bird of Paradise (Astrarchia stephaniae). Next, and perhaps the greatest thrill, came the Ribbon-tailed Bird of Paradise (Taenia paradisea mayeri), followed by the successes with the Golden-vented Bulbul (Pycnonotus goiavier person), Schalow's Touraco (Touraco schalowi), Striated Tanager (Thraupis bonariensis), and Amethyst Sunbird (Chalcomitra amethystina).

The following do not have the glamour of first successes, but are equally interesting. The Magnificent Bird of Paradise (Diphyllodes magnifica) now has five broods, totalling seven youngsters, and is, at present, residing over two eggs.

At far left:
Australian "White-browed
Wood Swallows," a first
breeding in America.
The parents are left
and right, the two
offsprings in the
center.

Middle: African
"White-cheeked
Touraco" with its two
week old youngling

A revelation was the latest breeding of the Imperial Fruit
Pigeon. The youngster of 1965 was permitted to stay with the
parents. The parents nested again in the early spring of 1966,
and after the hen had raised her first brood, the youngster of
1965 (which proved to be a female), proceeded to take over
the abandoned nest. After fertilization of her egg by her sire,
she hatched and reared her youngling, without any paternal
help. The new youngster now has fledged and is perfectly
normal in every visual aspect. As I write this, on 10th February, 1967, the original pair again has a youngster in the very
same nest.

In the case of the Stephanie's and the Ribbon-tailed
Birds of Paradise, hatching time was twenty-one days. Time
in the nest varied from twenty-two to twenty-six days. In
all nestings of the Stephanie's and Ribbon-tailed Birds of
Paradise, only one egg was laid.

Continued observation points up the lack of inclination
of Birds of Paradise to mate when the individuals have been
paired together for an extended period of time. New males,
or the same male, introduced just prior to the finishing of the
nest, are accepted for mating and copulation quite readily,
often instantaneously.

The pre-copulation ceremonies of the Stephanie are quite
vigorous and brutal; they grasp one another with their talons,

Right above: African
"White-breasted Rails"
bred in America for
the first time at the
Boehm Aviaries. The
young are coal-black
in their immature
plumage.

161

usually in the thighs, or in whatever manner chance may present. At times, it actually becomes "mortal combat," and I say this factually, because I have had hens kill glorious males. I do not wish to conjecture on how often death occurs, but we have lost two beautiful males in this manner, and I have been an observer of this combat on eight occasions. I have also seen a pair, in the throes of battle, fall into a pond of water. The birds would have drowned had they not been rescued. In all cases, their grasp on one another is so intent they fall to the ground; and they attack one another with their beaks. When the female is overpowered and becomes submissive they will then fly to a convenient branch where he will crest his hood and shield in a display of colour that is breathtaking! At the culmination of this display, copulation ensues.

"mortal combat"

Paradisea minor and Paradisea raggiana will display to each other, as well as to like species. Male displays are confined almost entirely to early morning or late evening activity. Of great interest is discovery of the fact that in the displays of Paradisea minor and Paradisea raggiana, the females take part, even when separated from the males. I have observed, day after day, the females displaying to one another in their abodes, or a female displaying to a male in view in an adjoining aviary. Male and female would cling to the wire separating the aviaries, or perch on branches as near to each other as could be achieved; dictated, of course, by

the growth of the trees in their respective confines. The female repeats the ritual of the male, who rhythmically and spherically umbrages his wings with a pulsation that carries no definable metre. He sends his plumes into a cascade so reminiscent of a waterfall. The female calls out as does the male, but in a much lower key, like the whining of a puppy; perhaps the begging of a fledgling for food would describe it better.

The females often display among themselves while the males are at rest. Their displays are of longer duration and shorter intervals than those of the males. My observations have not connected these displays with the nesting act, as I have had only one go to nest (Paradisea minor) and that was before I had pairs opposite to one another. I wonder if these complex displays are entirely a sexual attraction, or, rather, occasionally for amusement or play acting.

The Amethyst was our third success with Sunbirds, having bred the Scarlet-chested seven years ago, and the Golden-winged three years ago (although the young did not survive thirty days). We seem to have the greatest success in introducing Sunbirds to nest by starting a woven cocoon-like nest with heavy cord, weaving fine grasses between the meshes and then lining the inside with cotton. We hang the nest on the very tip of a tree branch. We then place in conspicuous places capok, wool, and dog hair for their choice. Horse-hair is occasionally used, but never before cutting it

"He sends his plumes into a cascade . . ."

From left to right above: Movements in the dance of the Lesser Bird of Paradise of New Guinea

into rather short lengths, as the long lengths can entwine their legs and wings, or enmesh them enough to hang themselves or make them vulnerable to attacks by other birds.

Eighteen days comprised the incubation period of the Amethyst Sunbird, twenty-one days the nest abode. The hen administered food entirely during the next period; however, the cock fed after the youngster had fledged. Ten days after the fledgling left the nest, the female re-laid and raised a subsequent chick—no animosity was displayed to the first chick by either parent after the arrival of the second chick.

The Striated Tanager raised two broods in 1966. These consisted of two in the first nest and one in the second. Two eggs were laid each time. Nest construction was similar to that of our Wood Thrush (Hylocichla mustelina), and was built in the very top of a white pine, 22 feet tall. The entire nest was of their own construction, and both male and female fed the young. At this writing, there seem to be two females and a male. Although the male has not yet come into mature colour (seven months of age), he is showing the colour patterns of a mature male, but in various shades of grey. The grey of the breast in the young male has a slight yellow-olive tint, indicating the brighter hue to come.

We have now a very comprehensive collection of New Guinea birds, consisting of pairs of Paradisea minor, Paradisea raggiana, Bluebird, Superb, Carol's, King's, Stephanie's, Ribbon-tailed, Sickle-bills, Magnificents, Orange-crested Bower Birds, Mackelot's Pitta, Hooded Pitta, Double-eyed Fig Parrots, Stella's Lorikeets—we have successfully reared the young of four species.

I should like to proffer an opinion concerning often-written articles about parents maliciously destroying their young, or casting them from the nest. The theory that malice prompts these actions is fallacious. I have occasionally seen it happen in our aviaries, but in each case, it was because the parents could not secure enough live food, particularly in the first one or two days of the chick's life. I know that many will say, "Well, I supplied this or that type of live food!" However, the questions to pose are: Was it of small enough size to suit the parent or parents? Were there other birds in the same aviary who might have depleted the supply before the parents could gather enough for the chicks, and before the attendant had returned with a fresh supply? Given a sufficient supply of live food, was there some environmental reason why the parents did not supply enough of it to the youngster?

I think few of us realize how many insects actually are fed in the course of a day. We know from experience it runs into hundreds per young. Many frugivorous, omnivorous, and seed-eating birds will not feed other than live insects until the young have left the nest or are well on their way to leaving it.

This is why I think many parents are unjustly accused of destroying their young. What they actually are doing, in my opinion, is removing the corpses from their nests preparatory to starting new nesting operations. I saw this happen recently when our female Amethyst raised two broods, the third being well into October. The chick was fifteen days old at the time, and we experienced a rather extended spell of rain. Food offerings were more than adequate, and the "black lights" were left on at night as usual. However, one has only to surmise that due to the rain falling, crepusculous, or night-flying insects, were not in their usual prevalence. Consequently, the chick died before the end of the second day. The parent removed the chick, but not before trying, in vain, to feed it throughout the afternoon on which it died.

It has been found here that the young among all types of birds raised in captivity are subject to rickets. Evidently the condition is brought about by the unavailability of insects containing chitinous or exoskeletal formation. We experienced it in starlings, touracos, tanagers, fairy bluebirds, etc. The parents will raise the young so affected; however, they are crippled for life and are best put down, as they can neither perch nor fly. Experiments were carried out in one case to see how long the parent would feed the affected youngster

African "Demoiselle Cranes" reside in "Lakeside Aviary."

that could not leave the nest area. Feeding was carried out over a longer period than with the normal chick who went on to fend for itself.

We have developed a positive preventive of rickets. Though simple in administration, it is, as far as I have been able to determine, 100 per cent effective. Preventive measures consist of taking a few drops of tasteless cod liver oil and rubbing them between the palms of the hands. Mealworms are then taken and similarly rubbed to give them a slight coating of cod liver oil. Care must be exercised not to overdo the oil application, as it apparently inhibits the breathing mechanism of the worms. This causes asphyxiation, and the birds are disinterested when the worms display no movement. A mixture of 75 per cent calcium carbonate, and 25 per cent steamed bone meal is prepared and placed in a large commercial-type salt shaker and kept at hand. After the application of the oil to the insects, they are dusted lightly with the above mixture. When the food is placed for the morning feeding, the shaker is carried along and a slight sprinkling applied directly to the food of that particular aviary. This method is essential and beneficial. When the mixture previously had been mixed into the bulk food formula, there were no visible beneficial results. Whether the calcium is lost by being absorbed by the fruit and food juices, I cannot yet determine. I do know, however, that if the direct application of the calcium is neglected on the insects or food of that aviary where the young is reared, we will experience rickets in the young.

The Schalow's Touraco reared two broods, although the first had to be destroyed because of rickets. The last brood came well into frost time, and before they were caught up to be placed in heated aviaries (the young at this time not being totally feathered), they were exposed to below-freezing temperatures, seemingly without any adverse effects. The parents did not seem to suffer any adverse effects either. The incubation period was the same as for all touracos, as was the length of stay in the nest.

The Schalow's make a much more elaborate nest than has been observed in other touraco species we have had. The nest is more "jay-like" in its construction. Not having experienced nesting preparations of all touraco species, I cannot say definitely that this is characteristic only of Schalow's.

Our "old faithfuls," the Fairy Wrens, Fairy Bluebirds, Natal Robin, and others previously reported, continue to be prolific. Most have raised two to three broods for the fourth consecutive year, and they are responsible for providing specimens to the San Diego, Washington, Cleveland, New York, and Brookfield Zoos. This tends to prove a long-held contention of the writer that a national or international aviary or aviaries could be established to propagate rare species and species in danger of extinction. Its feasibility would depend entirely on the people behind it—more definitely, on the men directly responsible for its every-day function.

I would suggest that all aviculturists give serious thought to such a possibility and, after a site were chosen and obtained, it could be built and maintained by an assessment to each zoological society in keeping with their available funds. Perhaps it could reach a status where government funds would be available for its use. I feel sure many pharmaceutical laboratories might be inclined to help support it, as it could well prove beneficial to their research programmes. Possibly some of the large foundations could lend support.

As the population continues to explode, there seems little doubt that flower and fauna will be taxed to their limits for survival. Will Rogers once said so aptly, on being asked what he liked most to invest his money in, "Real estate, 'cause that's one thing they 'aint' making any more of."

I expect to be in England some time in the coming year, when I will endeavour to meet as many aviculturists as time and occasion permit. If arrangements can be made at one of the meetings of the Avicultural Society, I should very much like to present a rather fascinating film. It has taken some months to prepare and bring to culmination. It will possess both sound and colour and will be made available for use by any Avicultural Society which desires to view it. It will show many first breedings and the various modes of parental care bestowed on the young by different species. Included will be incredibly beautiful displays by various species of the Birds of Paradise.

I should like, at this writing, to extend to all aviculturists interested in the propagation of birds, an invitation to visit the Boehm Aviaries, where appointments will be established by letter or phone. Some time in the near future, I will attempt an article on the relativity of area as a stimulus to birds to nest.

Edward Marshall Boehm
"The Avicultural Magazine"

The Edward Marshall Boehm
Hard-paste Porcelain Collection

*The Edward Marshall Boehm Collection spans a period
of twenty years and includes approximately 350
individual sculptures. If one were to take into account
the variations made on many of these sculptures
(different finishes, structural alterations and changes in
coloration), the total number of different pieces would
approximate 625.*

*In our studio collection we have a little better than half
of the sculptures. Early gallery samples often were sold
or given away. Some of the models which would not
sell and which, therefore, were not made in quantity
were accidentally damaged or otherwise lost over the
years.*

*A few notes about the collection. There are nine subject
categories. Each category is identified numerically and
by name. With the exception of sculptures for which*

no hallmark was assigned, subjects are numbered chronologically. Lack of assignment of hallmark numbers to certain sculptures was due to one or more of several factors: early introduction prior to adoption of a numbering system (in particular the dinnerware and many of the decorative sculptures); experimental pieces which were not intended for marketing (like the early Beau Brummells and the Blackburnian Warbler with Mountain Laurel); compositions made for specific occasions (the Angus Quads, the "Fabergé"-type egg); and many early sculptures which were "shelved" and not produced because they would not sell when introduced.

The reason Mr. Boehm made variations in size, color and finish was to help stimulate sales. The American Cocker, Boxer, Pope Pius XII, Swan and American Eagle are examples of sculptures made in two sizes. The Cocker provides an example of color changes as well. It was marketed in glazed, white and in five different color combinations. The Colt offered the greatest choice of colors. It was presented in bisque, white and in six decorations. The sculpture which best shows structural changes is the Thoroughbred. It was made five different ways by varying the combinations of key parts of the sculpture: the blanket, jockey and the exercise boy.

Four finishes were used: glazed, decorated; glazed, white; bisque, decorated; bisque, white. The first two primarily were used in the first few years of the studio. Gradually the latter two finishes were adopted almost entirely as Mr. Boehm concentrated increasingly on his bird sculpture. At present most of the work is completed in bisque, decorated.

The listing in the following pages is as complete as our present information allows. There are bound to be gaps and errors, some of which gradually will be corrected with the passage of time. A good part of the information was gathered previously in preparation for the Retrospective Exhibition held in 1964. Sources which contributed to this compilation are: Mrs. Boehm, our office staff and that of Reese Palley, our key artisans, old records and files, and collectors who own many of Mr. Boehm's early pieces.

Complete Listing...

COMPLETE LISTING...

● Dog Subjects

Hallmark Number	Subject	Finish
101	Boxer, large 9″ x 8½″	Glazed, Fawn / Glazed, Brindle
102	Boxer, small 5″ x 4½″	Glazed, Fawn / Glazed, Brindle
103	Scottish Terrier 6″ x 4½″	Glazed, Gray / Glazed, Black
104	American Cocker 6½″ x 5″	Glazed, Red / Glazed, Buff / Glazed, Black / Glazed, Brown and White / Glazed, Black and White / Glazed, White
104	Cocker, large	Glazed, Buff / Glazed, White
	American Cocker with Pheasant on base 7″ x 5″	Glazed, Brown and White
105	Wire Haired Fox Terrier 7″ x 6¼″	Glazed, decorated
106	Dane, reclining 10″ x 5½″	Glazed, Fawn / Glazed, Brindle / Glazed, Harlequin / Bisque, White
107	Great Dane 13″ x 12½″	Glazed, Fawn / Glazed, Brindle / Glazed, Harlequin / Glazed, White
108	Doberman Pinscher 9¼″ x 9¼″	Glazed, Black / Glazed, Red / Glazed, White
109	Standing Foxhound 9½″ x 9½″	Glazed, decorated
110	Reclining Foxhound 13¼″ x 6¼″	Glazed, decorated / Bisque, decorated / Bisque, White

Dog Subjects CONTINUED

Hallmark Number	Subject	Finish
129	German Shepherd 8″ high	Glazed, decorated
130	Pug 5″ high	Glazed, decorated / Bisque, White
131	English Bull Dog 7″ high	Glazed, decorated
132	Sheep Dog Pup 4½″ high	Bisque, decorated
133	French Poodle, reclining 5″ long	Bisque, decorated
	Skye Terrier	Glazed, decorated

● Cat Subjects

Hallmark Number	Subject	Finish
123	Cat with Two Kittens 5″ x 4″	Glazed, decorated / Bisque, decorated
124	Cat Playing with Ball 5½″ x 3″	Glazed, decorated

● Horses

Hallmark Number	Subject	Finish
201	Percheron Stallion 12″ x 9¼″	Glazed, Dapple Gray / Glazed, Dapple Gray with Roses / Glazed, Blue finish / Bisque, decorated / Bisque, White
202	Percheron Mare 11½″ x 8¼″	Glazed, decorated / Bisque, decorated / Bisque, White

No.	Item	Dimensions	Finishes
203	Hunter	14″ x 14″	Glazed, Dapple Gray / Bisque, Dapple Gray / Bisque, Bay
204	Colt	5¾″ x 6¼″	Glazed, Black / Glazed, Palomino / Glazed, Dapple Gray / Glazed, Black & White / Glazed, Brown & White / Glazed, Bay / Bisque, White
205	Arabian Stallions, pr.	10½″ x 7½″	Glazed, decorated / Bisque, decorated / Bisque, White
206	Polo Player	14″ x 13½″	Bisque, decorated
	Belgian Stallion	15″ x 12″	Glazed, decorated
	Percheron Mare & Foal on Base		Glazed, decorated
	Thoroughbred (No Blanket)	11″ x 7½″	Glazed, decorated
	Thoroughbred (With Blanket)	11″ x 7½″	Glazed, decorated / Bisque, decorated (Blanket glazed)
	Thoroughbred with Exercise Boy	11″ x 7½″	Glazed, decorated / Bisque, decorated
	Thoroughbred with Exercise Boy and Blanket	11″ x 7½″	Glazed, decorated
	Thoroughbred with Exercise Boy and Jockey	11″ x 10½″	Glazed, decorated / Bisque, decorated
	Thoroughbred Racing with Jockey	7″ x 5½″	Glazed, decorated / Bisque, decorated / Bisque, White

No.	Item	Dimensions	Finishes
111	French Poodle, standing	9″ x 7¾″	Glazed, Gray / Glazed, White / Glazed, Black / Glazed, Apricot
112	Springer	8½″ x 6¾″	Glazed, Liver & White / Glazed, Black & White
113	Beagle	7″ x 6¼″	Glazed, decorated / Glazed, White
114	Pointer	12½″ x 7″	Glazed, Liver & White / Glazed, Black & White
115	Bull Terrier	9½″ x 7½″	Glazed, White / Glazed, Brindle
116	Dachshund	9″ x 5″	Glazed, Tan / Glazed, Black & Tan / Glazed, White / Bisque, Tan
117	Labrador Retriever	9″ x 6¼″	Glazed, Black / Glazed, Lemon
118	Collie	10″ x 8½″	Glazed, Gold / Glazed, Tri-Colored / Glazed, White / Bisque, White
119	Greyhound, reclining	9″ x 5″	Glazed, decorated
120	Whippets, pr. on individual bases	7¾″ x 5½″	Bisque, White / Glazed, decorated
120	Whippet on base, large	18″ x 12″	Bisque, White
121	Pomeranian	4″ x 4″	Glazed, decorated
122	King Charles Spaniel	3″ x 3″	Glazed, decorated / Glazed, White
125	Yorkshire Terrier	3½″	Glazed, decorated
126	Dalmatian "Mike"	3″ x 1¼″	Glazed, decorated / Bisque, decorated
127	Basset Hound	7″ x 5¾″	Glazed, decorated / Bisque, decorated

Cattle Subjects

Hallmark Number	Subject	Finish
300	Holstein 16" x 9"	Glazed, decorated
301	Hereford Bull 10¼" x 5½"	Glazed, decorated Bisque, decorated Bisque, White
301	Hereford Bull on base	Glazed, decorated
302	Angus Bull 8¼" x 5"	Glazed, decorated Bisque, decorated
303	Shorthorn Bull 8½" x 5"	Glazed, Roan Glazed, Red Glazed, White
304	Brahman Bull 12" x 10"	Glazed, Gray Glazed, Red Glazed, White Bisque, White
305	Lamb 7½" x 4¼"	Bisque, decorated
	Quadruplet Black Angus Calves	Glazed, decorated

Bird Subjects

Hallmark Number	Subject	Finish
400	Wood Thrush with Crab Apple 8" x 5"	Glazed, decorated
401	Canvasback Ducks, pr. 4" high	Glazed, decorated Glazed, White Bisque, decorated
402	Green-Winged Teal, pr. 5" high	Glazed, decorated Glazed, White Bisque, decorated
403	Wood Duck, pr. 5" high	Glazed, decorated Bisque, decorated
	Wood Duck—male, only 5" high	Glazed, White Bisque, White
404	Leghorns, pr. 8" high	Glazed, decorated Bisque, White Bisque, decorated

Bird Subjects CONTINUED

Hallmark Number	Subject	Finish
419	Golden-Crowned Kinglets 11½" x 7½"	Bisque, White Bisque, decorated
421	Song Sparrows, pr. 17" high	Bisque, White Bisque, decorated
422	Carolina Wrens 14" x 10"	Bisque, White Bisque, decorated
423	Black-Tailed Bantams, pr. 13" high	Bisque, decorated
424	Cerulean Warblers, large 14" x 7¼"	Bisque, White Bisque, decorated
424	Cerulean Warblers, small 8" x 7¼"	Bisque, decorated
426	Red-Winged Blackbirds, pr. 17" high	Bisque, White Bisque, decorated
427	Downy Woodpeckers 13" x 5½"	Bisque, White Bisque, decorated
428	American Eagle, large 18" high	Bisque, White Bisque, decorated (eyes only)
428	American Eagle, small 15½" high	Bisque, White Bisque, decorated (eyes only)
429	Indigo Bunting 10" x 5½"	Bisque, White Bisque, decorated Bisque, decorated with Black Bases
429	Lazuli Bunting 10" x 5½"	Bisque, decorated
430	White-Throated Sparrow 9½" x 5¼"	Bisque, White Bisque, decorated Bisque, decorated with Black Bases
431	Yellow-Throated Warbler 10" x 5¼"	Bisque, White Bisque, decorated
432	Cedar Waxwing, Fledgling 3¼" x 2¾"	Bisque, White Bisque, decorated
433	California Quail, pr., large m. 9½" high, f. 9½" high	Bisque, White Bisque...

No.	Item	Finish
405	Red-Breasted Grosbeaks, pr. 6″ high	Glazed, decorated; Bisque, White
405	Evening Grosbeaks, pr. 6″ high	Bisque, decorated; Glazed, White (clay)
406	Mallards, pr. 11″ x 12″	Glazed, decorated
407	Bob White Quail, pr. m. 7″ high; f. 6″ high	Glazed, decorated; Glazed, decorated (with leaves applied); Bisque, White; Bisque, decorated
408	Canada Geese, pr. m. 7½″ high; f. 5½″ high	Glazed, decorated; Bisque, decorated; Bisque, White
409	Ring-Necked Pheasants, pr. m. 8″ high; f. 9″ high	Glazed, decorated; Bisque, White; Bisque, decorated
410	Gosling Duck 5″ x 2″	Glazed, decorated
411	Gun Stock Box with Mallards 7″ x 5″	Glazed, decorated
412	Chick 3½″ high	Glazed, decorated
413	Woodcock 9½″ x 10½″	Bisque, White; Bisque, decorated
414	Golden Oriental Pheasant 21″ x 6″	Bisque, White; Bisque, decorated
415	Cardinals, pr. m. 15½″ high; f. 10½″ high	Bisque, White; Bisque, decorated
416	Tumbler Pigeons, pr. 10″ x 4½″	Bisque, White; Bisque, decorated
417	Macaws, pr. 9″ high	Glazed, decorated; Glazed, White; Bisque, White
418	Cedar Waxwings, pr. m. 12″ high; f. 11½″ high	Bisque, White; Bisque, decorated

No.	Item	Finish
433	California Quail, pr., small m. 8½″ high; f. 7½″ high	Bisque, White; Bisque, decorated
434	Ruby-Crowned Kinglet 8″ high	Bisque, decorated
435	Meadowlark 8½″ x 7½″	Bisque, White; Bisque, decorated
436	Fledgling Blue Jay 4½″ x 3½″	Bisque, White; Bisque, decorated
437	Fledgling Robin 3½″ x 3¾″	Bisque, White; Bisque, decorated
438	Black-Capped Chickadee 9″ x 5½″	Bisque, White; Bisque, decorated
440	Hummingbird 8½″ x 5½″	Bisque, White; Bisque, decorated
441	Black-Throated Blue Warbler 10½″ x 5″	Bisque, White; Bisque, decorated
441	Blackburnian Warbler with Mountain Laurel 10½″ x 5″	Bisque, decorated
442	Fledgling Eastern Bluebird 4½″ x 3½″	Bisque, White; Bisque, decorated
443	Mourning Doves 14″ x 10″	Bisque, White; Bisque, decorated
444	Fledgling Wood Thrush (with Butterfly) 4½″ x 3½″	Bisque, White; Bisque, decorated
444	Fledgling Wood Thrush (with Insect)	Bisque, decorated
445	Prothonotary Warbler 5½″ x 6″	Bisque, White; Bisque, decorated
446	Nonpareil Bunting 8½″ x 5″	Bisque, White; Bisque, decorated
447	American Redstarts 11½″ x 6½″	Bisque, White; Bisque, decorated
448	Fledgling Goldfinch 4½″ x 3¾″	Bisque, White; Bisque, decorated

173

Bird Subjects CONTINUED

Hallmark Number	Subject	Finish
449	Fledgling Kingfisher 6" x 3¾"	Bisque, White / Bisque, decorated
450	Fledgling Purple Finches 4½" high	Bisque, White / Bisque, decorated
451	Eastern Bluebirds, pr. m. 14" high; f. 12" high	Bisque, White / Bisque, decorated
453	Owls, pr. 9" x 4"	Bisque, White / Bisque, decorated
456	Ruffed Grouse, pr. m. 12" high; f. 12" high	Bisque, White / Bisque, decorated
457	Goldfinches 11½" x 5½"	Bisque, White / Bisque, decorated
458	Fledgling Crested Flycatcher 5" x 3¼"	Bisque, White / Bisque, decorated
459	Mockingbirds, pr. m. 12½" high; f. 11½" high	Bisque, White / Bisque, decorated
460	Sugarbirds 25½" x 11"	Bisque, White / Bisque, decorated
461	Fledgling Chickadee 3¼" x 3¾"	Bisque, decorated
463	Ptarmigan, pr. m. 14" high; f. 9½" high	Bisque, White / Bisque, decorated
464	Lesser Prairie Chickens, pr. 10" high	Bisque, White / Bisque, decorated
466	Blue Jays with Chameleon, pr. m. 14" high; f. 12" high	Bisque, White / Bisque, decorated
467	Mearns' Quail, pr. m. 15" high; f. 7" high	Bisque, White / Bisque, decorated
468	Tree Sparrow 7½" x 6½"	Bisque, White / Bisque, decorated
469	Nuthatch 11" x 6"	Bisque, White / Bisque, decorated
470	Mountain Bluebirds 12" x 15"	Bisque, White / Bisque, decorated

Bird Subjects CONTINUED

Hallmark Number	Subject	Finish
492	Kestrels, pr. m. 14" high; f. 16½" high	Bisque, decorated
493	Road Runner 14" x 20½"	Bisque, decorated
494	Fledgling Western Bluebirds 6" x 4½"	Bisque, decorated
495	Fledgling Red-Poll 4" x 3¾"	Bisque, decorated
496	Mergansers, pr. m. 10½" high; f. 10½" high	Bisque, decorated
497	Common Tern 16" x 12"	Bisque, decorated

● Editions Introduced after January 29, 1969..

Hallmark Number	Subject	Finish
498	Young American Bald-Headed Eagle 9½" x 6"	Bisque, decorated
499	Fondo Marino 26" x 26"	Bisque, decorated
400-01	Western Bluebirds 17½" x 20"	Bisque, decorated
400-02	Verdins 8¾" x 6"	Bisque, decorated
400-03	Black-Headed Grosbeak 10" x 14½"	Bisque, decorated
400-04	Oven Bird 11" x 7"	Bisque, decorated
400-05	Adios 15" x 13¾"	Bisque, decorated / Glazed, decorated
400-06	Beau Brummells I (Evening Dress) m. 11½" high; f. 11½" high	Glazed, decorated

Number	Subject	Finish
471	Towhee 7½″ x 6¾″	Bisque, White / Bisque, decorated
472	Robin 13″ x 8″	Bisque, White / Bisque, decorated
473	Killdeer, pr. m. 9″ high; f. 8½″ high	Bisque, White / Bisque, decorated
475	Bobolink 14½″ x 8″	Bisque, White / Bisque, decorated
476	Fledgling Magpie 6″ x 3¾″	Bisque, decorated
478	Fledgling Blackburnian Warbler 4″ x 2½″	Bisque, White / Bisque, decorated
479	Fledgling Great Horned Owl 7″ x 5″	Bisque, White / Bisque, decorated
480	Ivory-Billed Woodpeckers 54″ high	Bisque, decorated
481	Varied Buntings 23″ x 14″	Bisque, decorated
482	Tufted Titmice 13″ x 6″	Bisque, decorated
483	Catbirds 14½″ x 7½″	Bisque, decorated
484	Parula Warblers 14½″ x 9″	Bisque, decorated
485	Wood Thrushes, pr. m. 16″ high; f. 15″ high	Bisque, decorated
486	Green Jays, pr. m. 18″ high; f. 14″ high	Bisque, decorated
487	Rufous Hummingbirds 14″ x 9″	Bisque, decorated
488	Crested Flycatcher 18½″ x 14″	Bisque, decorated
489	Blue Grosbeak 11″ x 10″	Bisque, decorated
490	Northern Water Thrush 10½″ x 8½″	Bisque, decorated
491	Fledgling Canada Warbler 8½″ x 8″	Bisque, decorated

Number	Subject	Finish
400-07	Beau Brummells II, (Daytime Dress) 11½″ high	Glazed, decorated
400-08	Edward Marshall Boehm Orchid 5″ x 8″	Bisque, decorated
400-09	Edward Marshall Boehm Orchid Centerpiece with Stellula calliope 17″ x 26″	Bisque, decorated
400-10	Baby Lazuli Buntings Paperweight 3½″ diameter	Bisque, decorated
400-11	Orchard Oriole 11″ x 14″	Bisque, decorated
	Hallmark Plaque (3,500 - used only for cover of limited edition book) 3½″ x 2″	Glazed, White with Gold "Boehm"

● *Wildlife Subjects*

Hallmark Number	Subject	Finish
501	Red Fox 6″ x 4″	Glazed, decorated / Glazed, White
502	Male Bunny 3″ x 3″	Glazed, decorated
503	Female Bunny 3″ x 2″	Glazed, decorated
504	Fawn 4″ x 3″	Glazed, decorated
505	Squirrel 2½″ x 2½″	Glazed, decorated / Glazed, White
506	Cub 5″ x 4½″	Glazed, decorated / Bisque, decorated
507	Lion 15″ x 6″	Glazed, decorated
508	Tiger 15″ x 6″	Glazed, decorated
509	Rabbit (with flowers on ribbon) 5″ x 4″	Bisque, White / Bisque, decorated

Religious Figures CONTINUED

Hallmark Number	Subject	Finish
619	Crucifix, Modern 36" high	Bisque, White (with Ebony Cross)
	Crucifix, Guido Reni 36" high	Bisque, White (with Ebony Cross)
		Bisque, White
620	Madonna and Child, Della Robbia 10" x 2"	Bisque, White
621	Pope John XXIII, Bust 10" high	Bisque, White
	Long Haired Angel	Glazed, decorated
	Madonna and Child	Glazed, decorated
		Glazed, White

● Decorative Pieces

Hallmark Number	Subject	Finish
701	Small Swan 4½" x 4"	Bisque, White
		Glazed, White
		Glazed, White with Gold Trim
702	Large Swan 8" x 7"	Bisque, White
		Glazed, White
		Glazed, White with Gold Trim
703	Fluted Grecian Vase 10" high	Glazed, decorated with Gold Trim
		Glazed, White
704	Ming Bowl Centerpiece 4¼" h. x 8½" diameter	Glazed, White
		Bisque, White
		Glazed, decorated
705	Oval Fluted Centerpiece, small 11" x 3"	Glazed, White
		Bisque, White
706	Oval Fluted Centerpiece, large 15½" x 7½"	Glazed, White
		Bisque, White
707	Fluted Cigarette Box 4¼" x 3"	Glazed, ground color body Pink

Wildlife Subjects CONTINUED

Hallmark Number	Subject	Finish
509	Rabbit (without flowers on ribbon) 5" x 4"	Bisque, decorated
510	White Mouse, Preening 2½" high	Glazed, decorated
		Bisque, decorated
511	Field Mouse with Vetch 4½" high	Bisque, decorated
		Bisque, White
512	Newborn Rabbits 8" x 4"	Bisque, decorated
513	Chipmunk 3½" high	Bisque, decorated
		Bisque, White
514	Chipmunk, Preening 3" high	Bisque, decorated
		Bisque, White
	Cottontail Bunny 6½" x 3¾"	Glazed, White

● Religious Figures

Hallmark Number	Subject	Finish
601	Madonna La Pieta, large 9½" high	Glazed, White
		Bisque, White
602	Small Madonna Bust 4½" high	Glazed, decorated with Gold Trim
603	Saint Maria Goretti 6½" high	Glazed, decorated
		Bisque, decorated
603	Saint Maria Goretti (same as above, but with feet closer together and flowers separate from body)	Glazed, decorated
604	Pigtail Angel 4½" high	Glazed, decorated
605	Madonna La Pieta, medium 6¼" high	Bisque, White
	Madonna Bust, medium 7" high	Glazed, decorated

No.	Item	Finish / Color
606	Lady of Grace 11¼″ high	Glazed, white / Bisque, White
607	Saint Joseph 15″ high	Glazed, decorated / Glazed, White / Bisque, White
608	Guardian Angel 7″ high	Glazed, decorated / Glazed, White / Bisque, White
609	Sister Angel (No drape on arms) 5″ high	Glazed, decorated / Bisque, White
609	Sister Angel (With drape on arms) 5″ high	Glazed, decorated / Bisque, White
610	Brother Angel (No drape on arms) 5″ high	Glazed, decorated / Bisque, White
610	Brother Angel (With drape on arms) 5″ high	Glazed, decorated / Bisque, White
611	Alba Madonna and Child 8″ high	Glazed, decorated / Glazed, White / Bisque, White
612	Saint Francis of Assisi 12½″ high	Bisque, White
612	Saint Francis of Assisi, small 7″ high	Glazed, Celadon
613	Madonna La Pieta, small 5″ high	Glazed, White / Bisque, White
614	Immaculate Conception 12″ high	Glazed, White / Bisque, White
615	Infant of Prague, Latin 10″ high	Bisque, White
615	Infant of Prague, Byzantine 10″ high	Bisque, White
618	Pope Pius XII Bust, large 14½″ high	Bisque, White
618	Pope Pius XII Bust, small 7½″ high	Bisque, White

No.	Item	Finish / Color
		Glazed, ground color body Celadon / Glazed, White
708	Small Ash Tray 3″ diameter	Glazed, White / Bisque, White
709	Fluted Candlesticks, pr., small 4″ high	Glazed, White
715	Bunny Box with Carrot 5″ x 4″	Glazed, decorated / Bisque, decorated / Glazed, White / Bisque, White
716	Tall Bunny Egg (Box) 8″ high	Glazed, decorated
717	Grape Jewel Box 5″ x 2½″	Bisque, White / Glazed, White
718	French Cachette 7″ x 5¼″	Bisque, White / Glazed, decorated with Gold Trim
720	Fluted Perfume Bottles, pr. 6½″ x 4½″	Glazed, White
720	Perfume Bottle, small 5″ high	Glazed, Yellow
721	Fluted Candy Box (Round) 6″ x 4½″	Glazed, White with Gold Trim
722	Corinthian Candlesticks, pr. 11½″ high	Glazed, White / Bisque, White
730	Bud Vase 3¼″ x 3″	Glazed, White / Bisque, White
735	Bunny Milk Mug 3¼″ high	Glazed, decorated
738	French Fluted Vase 10½″ high	Glazed, decorated with Gold Trim / Bisque, White
739	French Vase	Glazed, decorated / Bisque, White
741	Horse Head (bookends)	Glazed, decorated
742	Dolphin Shell Vase 7½″ high	Glazed, White / Bisque, White

Decorative Pieces CONTINUED

Hallmark Number	Subject	Finish
743	Bee Hive 5" high	Glazed, decorated
744	Empire Cachette 8" high	Glazed, decorated with Gold Trim
746	Bee Basket 3" x 2"	Glazed, decorated
		Bisque, White
		Bisque, decorated
747	Basket Centerpiece, oval 14" x 8½"	Glazed, White
		Glazed, decorated
		Bisque, White
748	Oval Grape Centerpiece 14" x 7½" x 6"	Glazed, decorated
		Glazed, White
		Bisque, White
749	Tulip Dinner Bell 4" high	Glazed, White
		Bisque, White
750	Tulip Vase 4¼" high	Glazed, decorated
		Glazed, White
		Bisque, White
751	Fruit Pyramid with Stand, pr. 13½" high	Glazed, decorated
		Bisque, White
752	Plain Urn 4½" high	Glazed, decorated with Gold Trim
		Glazed, White
		Bisque, White
752	Plain Urn, large 6¼" high	Glazed, White
753	Fluted Urn 4" high	Glazed, ground color body Pink
		Glazed, White with Gold Trim
		Bisque, White
		Glazed, ground color body Celadon
		Glazed, White
754	Small Fluted Ash Tray 3" diameter	Glazed, White
		Glazed, decorated with Gold Trim
		Bisque, White

Decorative Pieces CONTINUED

Hallmark Number	Subject	Finish
773	Traditional Centerpiece	Glazed, ground color body Celadon
		Glazed, White with Gold Trim
		Bisque, White
		Glazed with Black Trim
774	Traditional Candlesticks 4" high	Glazed, White
		Glazed, decorated
		Bisque, decorated
775	Modern Centerpiece 11" x 4"	Glazed, White
776	Triple Lotus Bowl	Bisque, White
777	Fluted Shell, small 5" high	Bisque, White
778	Fluted Shell, large 7" high	Bisque, White
779	Lotus Candlestick	Glazed, decorated
780	Cherub Nut Dish 5" x 11"	Bisque, White
	Tulip Bowl 7" x 4"	Glazed, White
		Bisque, White
	Grape Box with Two Cupids	Glazed, ground color body Pink
		Glazed, ground color body Celadon
	Fruit Bowl Set (1 large; 4 small)	Glazed, decorated
	Horn of Plenty	Glazed, decorated
	Tulip Vase, large 11" high	Glazed, White
		Glazed, decorated
	Lily Candelabra	Bisque, ground color body Pink
		Bisque, decorated
		Glazed, decorated
	Flower Vase 8¾" high	Glazed, White
		Glazed, decorated (falling leaves)
		Glazed, decorated (branch and blossoms)
		Glazed, decorated (ferns)
		Glazed, White

No.	Item	Description
	Ornate Urn 9" high	Glazed, White
	Bird Urn 11½" high	Glazed, decorated (green parakeets) / Glazed, decorated (water lilies) / Glazed, decorated (raised leaves and cockatoos) / Glazed, White / Glazed, decorated
	Swan Cake Plate 15½" x 11½"	Glazed, White / Glazed, Pink
	Crimped Bowl 5" diameter	Glazed, White with Gold Trim
	Crimped Candy Dish 5" diameter	Glazed, White / Glazed, Pink
	Crimped Vase 6½" high	Glazed, White
	Oval Fluted Candlestick 3⅓" x 3"	Bisque, White
	Thin-necked Vase 8" high	Glazed, White / Bisque, White
	Shell Platter 10" diameter	Glazed, decorated
	Three-Section Nut Dish	Glazed, White
	Ribbed Vase 6½" high	Glazed, White / Glazed, ground color Celadon
	Round Ash Tray, large 4" diameter	Glazed, White / Glazed, decorated
	Rectangular Fluted Ash Tray 3" long	Glazed, decorated
	Holly Tray 13" diameter	Bisque, White / Glazed, White with Gold Trim / Glazed, Pink / Glazed, Celadon
	Fluted Nut Dish 5" diameter	Glazed, White
	Bell Candlestick 5¼" high	Glazed, White
	Planter 5¾" high	

No.	Item	Description
755	Clover Cigarette Box 5" high	Glazed, decorated / Bisque, decorated
756	Acorn Cigarette Box 5" high	Glazed, decorated / Bisque, decorated
757	Cigarette Set, Medallion	Glazed, decorated
758	Shell Flower Holder 5" high	Glazed, White / Bisque, White
759	Half-Fluted Ash Tray 3" diameter	Glazed, White / Bisque, White
760	Chinese Vase 9" high	Glazed, decorated / Glazed, White / Bisque, White
761	Grape Candlesticks, pr. 7½" high	Glazed, White / Bisque, White
762	Maple Leaf Ash Tray 4" x 3"	Bisque, White / Bisque, decorated
764	Lotus Bowl, large 7" diameter	Glazed, White / Bisque, White
764	Lotus Bowl, small 4½" diameter	Glazed, White / Bisque, White
765	Muffineer 5" high	Glazed, White / Glazed, decorated / Glazed, White with Gold Trim
766	Ming Candlesticks, pr. 4" diameter	Bisque, White
767	Fluted Cigarette Box	Glazed, White with Gold Trim
768	Clover Ash Tray 4" diameter	Glazed, White / Glazed, decorated
769	Acorn Ash Tray 4" diameter	Glazed, White / Glazed, decorated / Bisque, decorated
770	Grecian Candy Box	Glazed, decorated / Glazed, White
771	Fluted Candlesticks, pr., large 5" high	Bisque, White
772	Shell Nut Dish 5" x 4¼"	Glazed, White / Glazed, ground color body Pink

Decorative Pieces *CONTINUED*

Hallmark Number	Subject	Finish
	Tulip Candlestick 4″ high	Bisque, White
	Round Fluted Candlesticks 5″ diameter	Bisque, White
	Easter Egg Paperweight	Glazed, decorated Bisque, White
	Candy Egg	Glazed, decorated
	Round Fluted Ash Tray 3¾″ x 1″	Glazed, White with Gold Trim Bisque, White Glazed, Celadon
	Vase with Drape	Glazed, decorated-Pink Glazed, decorated with Gold Trim
	Ring-Top Vase 15″ high	Glazed, White
	Tulip Nutmeg Shaker	Glazed, decorated
	Egg ("Faberge"-style)	Glazed, decorated

● Pitchers

Hallmark Number	Subject	Finish
801	Rose Pitcher 7″ high	Glazed, White Bisque, White Glazed, decorated
802	Tulip Pitcher 6½″ high	Glazed, White Glazed, decorated Bisque, White
803	Grape Pitcher 8½″ high	Glazed, decorated—Blue Grapes Glazed, decorated—Natural Grapes Glazed, decorated—Purple Grapes Bisque, White
804	Holly Pitcher 7½″ high	Glazed, decorated Glazed, decorated—Blue

● Figurine Subjects *CONTINUED*

Hallmark Number	Subject	Finish
910	Ballerina, Swan Lake 7½″ high	Glazed, decorated Bisque, decorated Bisque, White
911	Cherub on Pedestal 5½″ high	Bisque, White
912	Beau Brummells, pr. 12″ high	Glazed, decorated Bisque, White
	Gay Nineties, pr. 8″ high	Glazed, decorated Glazed, White Bisque, decorated
	Mischief 5″ high	Glazed, decorated
	Innocence 5″ high	Glazed, decorated
	Ballerina, Pinky 5½″ high	Bisque, decorated
	Ballerina, Pamela 6½″ high	Bisque, decorated
	Dutch Boy and Girl, pr., large	Glazed, decorated
	Dutch Boy and Girl, pr., small (Salt & Pepper Shakers)	Glazed, decorated
	Ichabod Crane 7½″ high	Glazed, decorated
	Bathing Beauty	Glazed, White
	Susie (Lipstick Girl) 7″ high	Glazed, decorated
	Choir Boy 4½″ high	Glazed, decorated
	"Trilafon" Phrenology Head 5¼″ high	Glazed, Head sectionalized by black lines
	"Etrafon" Phrenology Head 5¼″ high	Glazed, Head sectionalized by incised lines

● Dinnerware

Hallmark Number	Subject	Finish
	Service Plates 10" diameter	Glazed, decorated (Wild Flowers)
	Demi-Tasse Cups 2½" high	Glazed, decorated (Wild Flowers); Glazed, decorated (Gold Flowers on Black Background)
	Demi-Tasse Cups on Base 4" high	Glazed, decorated; Glazed, ground color body Pink; Glazed, ground color body Celadon
	Teacup and Saucer	Glazed, decorated (Wild Flowers)
	After Dinner Cups 3¾" x 3"	White, Gold trim
	Gravy Boat	Glazed, White; Bisque, White
805	Holly Cups 2½" high	Glazed, decorated; Glazed, decorated—Blue
806	Tulip Pitcher 7½" high	Glazed, decorated; Glazed, White
807	Tulip Cups	Glazed, decorated
808	Holly Nutmeg Shaker 2¼" high	Glazed, decorated
810	Rose Coffee Pot 10½" high	Glazed, White; Bisque, White
811	Rose Sugar Bowl 5" high	Glazed, White; Bisque, White
812	Rose Creamer 4½" high	Glazed, White; Bisque, White

● Figurine Subjects

Hallmark Number	Subject	Finish
901	Neptune with Seahorse 7" x 5½"	Bisque, decorated; Bisque, White
902	Diana with Fawn 7" x 5½"	Bisque, decorated; Bisque, White
903	Venus 8" high	Bisque, decorated; Bisque, White
904	Mercury 7¼" x 4"	Bisque, decorated; Bisque, White
905	Apollo 7¼" x 3½"	Bisque, decorated; Bisque, White
906	Quan Yin 16" high	Glazed, White; Bisque, White
907	Cupid with Flute 5¼" high	Glazed, decorated; Bisque, decorated; Bisque, White
908	Cupid with Harp 5½" high	Glazed, decorated; Bisque, decorated; Bisque, White
909	Cupid with Horn 5¼" high	Glazed, decorated; Bisque, decorated; Bisque, White

"Wood Thrushes" designed by Edward Boehm and his artisans.
A limited issue service plate produced by Lenox, Inc., on Lenox china.
Introduced in 1970

LIMITED
EDITIONS
from 1961 . . .

Goldfinches with Scottish Thistle

(Astragalinus tristis tristis)   PLATE 1

The abandon and wild delight of the procrastinating Goldfinch, during the season when other birds are busily feeding their young, have labelled him as the "playboy" among our feathered friends. A late nester, the Goldfinch frolics and sings with an ecstasy which carries him off his feet, and he circles over the fields sowing the air with his gay music. He seems to be saying to his hard-working cousins, "I have made a long and tiring trip; so for a while I am going to play and sing in the sunshine and I shall tend to my chores later."

After most of the other birds are through with their nesting, and all of the others have already begun, the Goldfinch turns his attentions to his mating responsibilities and gathers thistledown and fine grasses for the nest in a low, shaded bush. While hard at work, he retains his gay disposition; and there are few prettier sights than to watch him fluttering along a hedge, chasing the thistledown as it is whirled around by the breeze, and uttering all the while his merry notes: per-chic-o-ree, per-chic-o-ree. . . .

The adult male and female Goldfinches of the sculpture are with Scottish thistle. In summer the male's body has a brilliant lemon-yellow and the wings and tail are black. In winter he dons a plumage similar to that of the female's year-around dress. The upper parts become olive-brown, the under parts yellow-gray. As recreated in the sculpture, the stubby, cone-shaped beak, indicative of a seed-eater, long and pointed wings, short legs, and short, forked tail are characteristic of the Finch family, the largest family of birds in the world.

Other Names: "Willow Goldfinch;" "Pale Goldfinch;" "Thistle Finch."

Distribution: From southern Canada south to northern South America.

State Bird of: New Jersey, Washington, Minnesota and Iowa.

PLATE 1

Size of Sculpture: Height 11 inches; Width 5 inches.

A limited edition of 500 replicas.

Issued in 1961

PLATE 2

The Mockingbird sculptures introduced a new technique. The bindweed blooms, permanently affixed to fine metal stems and stamens, are detachable from the two figures. The artist designed the pair in this manner because of the nature of this beautiful flower. Bindweed has an extremely thin bloom and it grows at the end of a long, thin stem which is its lone support. In order to effect the natural free growth of the bindweed in the sculptures and to reduce the possibility of breakage in transportation, Mr. Boehm introduced metal components into the composition.

The Mockingbird is an easy bird to recognize in nature. He is graceful and slender with slate-gray back and light underparts. When in motion he exhibits a large amount of white in his wings and tail. As a songster he is unrivaled; and his delightful chatter leads one to believe that he may be the happiest of all our birds. He equals and even excels the whole feathered choir, and it is reported he can mimic any sound if he puts his mind to it. He is found often as far north as the New England States but his regular areas are the southeastern and southcentral regions of our country.

Other Names: Mock Bird; Mocking Thrush; Mimic Thrush; Mocker.

State Bird Of: Arkansas, Florida, Mississippi, Tennessee, Texas.

Size of Sculptures: Male Height 12½ inches; Width 7 inches.

Female Height 11½ inches; Width 6 inches.

A limited edition of 500 pairs.

Issued in 1961

Sugarbirds

(Cyanerpes cyaneus)

PLATE 3

The porcelain sculpture "Sugarbirds" is one of the largest and most intricate Boehm porcelain figures. It features two pairs of exotic birds, Yellow-winged Sugarbirds and Purple Sugarbirds, in various postures of flight and rest about the main stump. The respective mates are identified by similarity of foot color. The foliage sprouting from the main stump includes philodendron, ferns and cypripedium orchids. The transference of the original sculpture into porcelain required the construction of approximately 600 mold parts. Like the flowers of the "Mockingbird" sculptures, the orchid flowers are set to metal stems and are removable.

The male Sugarbirds display varying shades of purple, yellow and blue. The females predominantly are moss green. These little guests whose homelands extend from northern Mexico south to Brazil act and live much like our hummingbirds. They belong to the group of birds known as honey creepers, which are small, usually brilliantly colored, and found only in subtropic and tropic America.

Size of Sculpture: Height 25 inches; Width 10 inches.

A limited edition of 100 replicas.

Issued in 1961

PLATE 3

189

PLATE 4

Size of Sculpture: Male Height 14 inches; Width 10 inches.
Female Height 9½ inches; Width 12 inches.

A limited edition of 350 pairs.

Issued in 1962

Ptarmigan

PLATE 4

(Lagopus lagopus lagopus)

The extreme northern portion of North America is the home of the Ptarmigan, a gallinacious member of the feathered world. He is characterized by his terrestrial nature, protective seasonal variations in color, feathered legs and toes for these parts to endure the northern temperatures, and a distinct red brow, in the shape of a quarter-moon, above the eyes of the male. This well-known Arctic inhabitant is the state bird of Alaska. In some areas he also is called "Rock Ptarmigan" and "Snow Grouse."

The porcelains present the Ptarmigan in their winter plumage. The predominantly pure white dress blends with the snowy background of their habitat and serves to diffuse their presence to even the most discerning eye. In the spring of each year new plumage, grouse-like in appearance, is donned in protective conformity with warm weather surroundings.

A unifying center rock is part of the porcelain composition. It may be used to "join" the male and female sculptures into a centerpiece; or, the two may be separated from the center rock and shown as a pair.

Lesser Prairie Chickens

(Tympanuchus pallidicinctus)

PLATE 5

The Lesser Prairie Chicken, also named "Prairie Hen," "Pinnated Grouse" and "Prairie Grouse," once was widespread in central and southcentral parts of the United States. He now is nearly extinct. Hunters and domesticated animals have helped decimate his numbers, but his greatest losses have been due to the destruction of his natural foods and covers by the ever-encroaching grain farmers.

The artist depicted the birds in a pose for which they are most well known, the posture and action of their remarkable mating performance. During the season from March to early May, ten to fifty gathered in an area before daybreak to perform rituals. The hens glibly strolled about in the courtship area. The males, in an attempt to arouse the females, engaged in gaudy tournaments of display and combat. The feather-tufts on the neck were erected like horns, the tail raised and spread, the wings drooped, when the bird first rushed forward a few steps, paused, inflated its orange-like air sacs, and with a violent, jerking, muscular effort, produced the startling boom-ah-b-o-o-m, boom-ah-b-o-o-m, which may have been heard two miles away. When he came within striking distance of a rival exhibitionist, a tense struggle would ensue resulting in a clashing of wings and the loss of many feathers. After an hour or two, depending on the ardor of the birds, the competition for the day would be over.

PLATE 5

Size of Sculpture: Male Height 10 inches; Width 12 inches.

Female Height 10 inches; Width 8 inches.

A limited edition of 300 pairs.

Issued in 1962

PLATE 6

Size of Sculpture: Male Height 14 inches; Width 10 inches.

Female Height 12 inches; Width 12 inches.

A limited edition of 250 pairs.

Issued in 1962

194

Blue Jays With Young and Chameleon

PLATE 6

(Cynocitta cristata cristata)

The clown and scoffer of the bird world is the Blue Jay. Furthermore, he is a definite rascal and, in the opinion of many who know the bird well, has all of the mischievous, thieving traits of the crow—with a lot of audacity thrown in. His good traits are not manifest usually because of an obstreperous, noisy demeanor. Yet, let alone its beauty, vegetable foods are from wild sources and a good part of the diet consists of noxious insects harmful to the farmer. Kleptomaniacal and hiding propensities also serve a useful purpose. As with the squirrel, they result in dissemination of seeds of future chestnut and oak trees. The range of the Blue Jay is temperate eastern North America. Other names given it are "Blue Coat," "Jay" and "Common Jay."

The artist sculptured the Blue Jays in family, showing the great devotion to familial responsibilities the adults possess. The setting is of old stumps on which the Jays have settled. The female, who appears always to be gathering food, finds one youngling contented and asleep, and so prepares to feed the other which has not had its fill. Nearby the male protector, in his harsh manner, is engaged in frightening off a curious chameleon.

Mearns' Quail

(Cyrtonyx montezumae mearnsi)   PLATE 7

Mearns' Quail, like many other unfortunate species, has suffered near-extinction. They are common nowhere in the
United States, excepting the birds owned by breeders. Although his true home is in the arid regions of the southwestern
part of our country, fortunately the habits and food of this
quail vary considerably and he is adaptable to taming and to
cultivated areas. With proper care and attention, perhaps one
day he again may grace our fields and prairies. Part of the
blame for his scarcity must lie with this bird's disposition.
He is a quiet, peaceful, confiding bird and, like some of his
relatives, has earned the common name of "Fool Hen" by
allowing himself to be killed with a stick or stone.

The artist provided an indigenous arid setting for the
Mearns' Quail. Their coloring is in some ways similar to the
Bob White; but the male is unmistakable by its clown-like,
white-marked face and the pattern of white dots which pocks
the black breast and flanks. While her mate prepares to
capture an unsuspecting "Tiger Beetle," the more somberly-
colored female hovers over her two young. The beetle of the
sculpture has a lustered porcelain body and oxidized gold
appendages.

PLATE 7

Size of Sculpture: Male Height 15 inches; Width 9 inches.
Female Height 7 inches; Width 7 inches.
A limited edition of 350 pairs.
Issued in 1963

PLATE 8

Size of Sculpture: Height 12 inches; Width 15 inches.

A limited edition of 300 replicas.

Issued in 1963

PLATE 8

(Sialia currucoides)

The Mountain Bluebird (also called Arctic Bluebird) is a member of the large, cosmopolitan Thrush family. Although he is slightly larger, this Bluebird presents an appearance generally similar to that of his eastern relative. As indicated by his name, he makes his home in the mountain districts of western North America—and at unusually high altitudes. Observers have reported sighting families of them in the Rocky Mountains above timber lines to approximately 13,000 feet. His diet consists mainly of insects, with minor amounts of fruit. He has been named the state bird of Idaho and Nevada.

The artist presented the Mountain Bluebirds with flowering magnolia. The male sits high on a branch above his mate. The female differs slightly in color, with less brilliant blues of the back and with under parts predominantly brownish-gray to white. Both show a posture of activity characteristic of the species.

Towhee

The habitats of the Towhee are in the eastern and east-central parts of the United States. Because of his unusual song, habits and rather widespread distribution, he has perhaps been given more names than any member of the Finch family. The more common ones are "Chewink," "Bullfinch" and "Red-eyed Towhee." Among his peculiar characteristics are his ventriloquistic faculty, his apparent lack of concern when his terrestrial nest is approached, and his ground-foraging with his feet—after the manner of the domesticated hen. As with most finches, seeds and insects are his principal foods, and he shows an occasional fondness for wild fruits of all kinds.

The male Towhee of the sculpture is among fall-fruiting mushrooms. His coloring varies from black upper parts to brownish and white under parts. The strong, cone-shaped bill indicates his finch-like propensity for seeds. Other identifying features are his short, rounded wings, stout feet and red iris of the eye.

Size of Sculpture: Height 8 inches; Width 8 inches.

A limited edition of 500 replicas.

Issued in 1963

PLATE 9

PLATE 10

Robin

PLATE 10

(Planesticus migratorius migratorius)

The best known, and one of the best loved, birds of America is the Robin. He is the state bird of Connecticut, Michigan and Wisconsin—indicative of his widespread distribution. He is one of our important spring harbingers, exhibits a great fondness for human society and has a conspicuous plumage. His chief rival in these respects is his cousin, the Bluebird; but the Robin is more characteristic of the two and much more in evidence because of his propensity for our lawns and the trust he displays when building his nest and rearing his young. Perhaps overpraise has been given the Robin's song. It is cheerful rather than melodious, bright and incisive rather than musical. Ascending and descending phrases often terminate on a discordant note—much like a break in the tones of a young lad whose voice is changing.

In porcelain the male Robin, in his spring suit, is presented terrestrially among daffodils. Nearby sits a snail—probably wondering at its neighbor's song. As shown by the sculpture, features identifying the Robin as a member of the Thrush family are his bill, curving slightly downward and decidedly shorter than the head; wings rather long and pointed, and a broad tail which is shorter than the wing.

Size of Sculpture: Height 13 inches; Width 8 inches.

A limited edition of 500 replicas.

Issued in 1964

Killdeer

(Oxyechus vociferus)   PLATE 11

The Killdeer is a Plover. Unlike most shore birds, he often travels far inland and supplements his diet by feeding on worms, grubs and bugs. His nervous manner and petulant cry of "kill-dee, kill-dee" may be heard throughout his range in the Western Hemisphere. The Killdeer is especially solicitous about his young. When threatened, one of the parents will resort to the tactics of ground-building birds, fluttering away from the family with wings dragging as if injured, huffing and puffing and keeping up a raucous screaming. Meanwhile, the other parent stealthily will lead the young to safety among the underbrush.

The sculptures depict this injury-feigning act with the male the actor. The female, similar in color to her mate, leads the young to protective cover—bending, in the hurry, the delicate bluebells. Prominent characteristics of the Killdeer are the black bands of the breast, long rounded tail, slender bill and long wings which, in flight, show a white "V."

PLATE 11

Size of Sculpture: Male Height 9 inches; Width 12 inches.
Female Height 8½ inches; Width 12 inches.
A limited edition of 300 pairs.
Issued in 1964

PLATE 12

Bobolink

PLATE 12   *(Dolichonyx oryzivorus)*

The Bobolink, affectionately called "Robert," inhabits eastern and central temperate North America. He is loved as the flamboyant, handsome, frolicking minstrel of the meadows. Spontaneity of action and infectious mirth describe his demeanor. His song is so frenzied and varied it is virtually impossible to render; and "bobolink, bobolink, spink, spank, spink" is a much simplified interpretation. Often while on the wing, the Bobolink is likely to suddenly become a whole symphonic orchestra bursting with sound and gaiety and looking as though he is about to explode into a cloud of feathers and song.

The artist's Bobolink, a male in his best spring suit, is in a farmer's field—having selected winter-worn corn stubble from which to pour forth his song. His impressively-outlined uniform is in sharp contrast to the dull, mottled appearance brought by his fall molt. His wings are long and pointed, the tail shorter than the wing—with stiff, abruptly tapering feathers—and his bill is conical and sharp.

Size of Sculpture: Height 14½ inches; Width 8 inches.

A limited edition of 500 replicas.

Issued in 1964

Fledgling Great Horned Owl

(Bubo virginianus virginianus)   PLATE 13

"Tiger of the airways" is an apt description of the Great Horned Owl. Throughout his range in eastern North America the big bird (adult size to twenty-four inches in length) is well known for his daring and powerful hunting ability. To the poultry farmer this owl can be a veritable terror; but he has a capacity for good works, too, as he is the important nocturnal enemy of rodents. Like other raptorial birds, owls are wonderfully equipped with powerful talons and flight, lightning swiftness and superb vision. The bird's breeding habits are peculiar. The eggs, normally two, are laid before March—sometimes as early as late January. It is not uncommon to find a female stolidly incubating under a blanket of snow. When the young are old enough to balance themselves, the parents immediately destroy the large, conspicuous nest thus leaving the younglings well protected by the harmony of their colors with their natural surroundings.

The age of the sculpted owl would be four to six weeks, about the time when he would begin to don his adult coloring and conspicuous horn-like tufts of feathers. The rounded face, large eyes and tufts are responsible for his common name of "Cat Owl." Other names are "Big Hoot Owl," "Virginia Owl" and "Virginia Horned Owl." The sexes usually are colored alike. However, in many individuals the color is dichromatic; and, wholly independent of sex or age, they may differ remarkably in coloration. The extreme color phases range from gray or brownish-gray to cinnamon-rufous or ocherous.

Size of Sculpture: Height 7 inches; Width 5 inches.

A limited edition of 750 replicas.

Issued in 1965

PLATE 13

PLATE 14

Varied Buntings

PLATE 14

(Passerina versicolor versicolor)

Perhaps the most beautiful of all Buntings, and one of the most beautiful of all birds of America, is the little-known Varied. He is a quiet-mannered bird located in the sparsely-populated areas of the southeastern and southcentral areas of the United States. Even the expert bird-watcher is hard put to spot one as he confines his activities to dense river-bottom thickets and the tangled brush of steep hillsides. This species is one of about two hundred of the great Finch Family in our country. The vernacular name, "Bunting," means plump or dumpy and refers to the stocky little bodies of its members. The song of the Varied is sweet and concise but feeble and much inferior to that of the Indigo. As with all Finches, he is an extremely useful bird, for his diet consists almost wholly of weed seeds.

The floral setting in the porcelain composition is the spectacular "Fritillaria imperialis," or "Crown Imperial," of the Lily family. It is a spring-blooming plant having at the top of the single stalk a cluster of pendant, bell-shaped flowers surrounded by a whorl of leaves. The stalk and flower stems of the sculpture are fashioned of metal. The male Varied Bunting, in his startling wine-red and wine-lavender coat, is attempting to draw the attention of his modestly-attired mate. Like most strikingly-garbed males, he will strut and parade for long periods for his pleasure as well as the female's.

Size of Sculpture: Height 23 inches; Width 14 inches.

A limited edition of 300 replicas.

Issued in 1965

Tufted Titmice

(Baeolophus bicolor) PLATE 15

The Tufted is a member of the Titmouse Family which comprises several species of small birds. Like his equally-loved cousin, the Chickadee, he is predominantly a bird of the eastern United States—but he often is seen in the southern and southcentral areas of our country as well. Apart from his numbers, he is well known for his good looks, boldness, pertness and curiosity. Non-migratory, the Tufted is seen throughout his wide range in all seasons of the year. In winter he bands into little flocks of a dozen or more, each band usually representing a family of parents and their two broods of the year. No ill will should exist for the Tufted. The character of his diet, alone, earns great respect, for it consists largely of insects in warm seasons and of the eggs and larvae of these pests in winter. Other names given this bird are "Tufted Tit," "Tufted Chickadee," "Crested Titmouse," "Peto Bird" and "Crested Tomtit."

The Tufted Titmice of the sculpture are frolicking about the snow-laden sumac panicles. Their postures indicate their concise, acrobatic antics. Male and female of the species are similar in color and size. The primary identifying feature is their somewhat exaggerated head crests. Other characteristics of this family are short, cone-shaped bills, long and rounded wings, and short, slightly-rounded tail.

Size of Sculpture: Height 13 inches; Width 6 inches.

A limited edition of 500 replicas.

Issued in 1965

PLATE 15

PLATE 16

Catbird

PLATE 16

(Dumetella carolinensis)

There is more of the cat about the Catbird than his cat-like call, as evidenced by his unpopularity among other birds. Besides his ability to snarl, his manners are distinctly feline and his habit of slinking through brushes and snooping among the nests of his neighbors reaps deserved suspicion. In spite of his "exile," he constantly exhibits a proud individuality and brashness, and no other bird works harder at "showing off" to all who will turn a head. All of this is a pity, as the Catbird is a distinct, amusing and interesting personality among bird life. His clever posing and attitudinizing, versatility and imaginative vocal potpourri mark him an intelligent species. His range is Temperate North America, west of the Rocky Mountains. Other names are "Chicken Bird," "Cat Fly-catcher," "Slate-colored Mockingbird" and "Black-capped Thrush."

Were he able to speak, no doubt the histrionic Catbird would express pleasure to the artist for being cast in porcelain among hyacinths—in classic mythology a flower which sprang from the blood of the beautiful youth Hyacinthus at the command of the bereaved Apollo. With his abilities as a member of the Mimic Thrush Family, this bird could bring into play for his setting appropriate orchestral instruments and movements; for, like his closest relative, the Mockingbird, the Catbird is capable of clearly rendering the more difficult tones of the flute, piccolo, violin and cello.

Size of Sculpture: Height 14½ inches; Width 7½ inches.

A limited edition of 500 replicas.

Issued in 1965

Parula Warblers

(Compsothlypis americana americana)   PLATE 17

The name "Parula," which means diminutive Parus or Titmouse, was given to this beautiful American Warbler because of his Chickadee-like habits in his search for food. He often is seen hanging under a limb, with nimbleness and agility, while he feeds. But his distinctive, soft coloring allows quick identification, and some of his "local" names are descriptive of his coloring: "Blue Yellow-Backed Warbler;" "Blue Yellow-back;" "Finch Creeper;" "Southern Parula Warbler." The species, limited to the eastern half of the United States, may be divided into northern and southern Parulas, overlapping in New Jersey and Maryland. The northern variety is slightly larger and his coloring richer. Hanging moss is the preferred nesting material and site of the bird. He cleverly interweaves the moss, adding enough soft plant material to make a comfortable, safe bottom for the nest.

Both male (in the high position) and female Parula Warblers of the sculpture are shown in postures of great activity in their pursuit of food—their attentions focused on a butterfly and lady bug. The female is the same size as the male and the coloring is similar but duller. Prime Warbler characteristics are the short, narrow, wedge-shaped bill, long wings and forked tail. Winding about the weathered fence post are wild morning glories of the variety Ipomoea digitata.

Size of Sculpture: Height 14½ inches; Width 9 inches.

A limited edition of 400 replicas.

Issued in 1965

216

PLATE 17

Wood Thrushes

(Hylocichla mustelina)

PLATES 18 · 19

The Thrush clan is one of the most diversified in respect to appearance, habits, form and coloration. Its family scope in the United States can be defined generally by the more domesticated, colorful "Robin" and "Bluebirds" to the rarely-seen, less colorful, shy cousins of the forests—the "Hermit," "Olive-backed," "Veery," etc. The Wood Thrush is unique. Although deep woods are his natural and generally-preferred habitat, he frequently makes his home quite near us. His range is eastern temperate North America in summer to Central America in winter. Many would argue that the Wood Thrush is the handsomest member of his tribe and the best songster.

All would agree that he has the most elegant manners. His other names are "Song Thrush," "Wood Robin," "Bell Bird" and "Swamp Robin." He is the official bird of the District of Columbia.

The male of the sculptures, as he often does, has paused from his family duties to revel in song. His mate busily attends to three hungry younglings whose bright gullets stimulate the parents to gather food tirelessly. The setting is a profusion of sweet azaleas (Rhododendron arborescens), the stamens of which have been formed from fine metal. The birds vary, as adults, from seven to eight inches. Male and female generally are identical in size and coloration.

Size of Sculptures:
Male Height 16 inches; Width 11 inches.
Female Height 15 inches; Width 15 inches.
A limited edition of 400 pairs.
Issued in 1966

219

PLATE 20

Size of Sculptures: Male, Height 18 inches; Width 12 inches.
Female, Height 14 inches; Width 10 inches.

A limited edition of 400 pairs.

Issued in 1966

Green Jays

PLATE 20

(Cyanocorax yncas)

The Green Jay is found chiefly in southeastern Texas and Mexico. His limited range in the United States is indicated by his local Texas name, "Rio Grande Green Jay." The Mexicans call him "Pajaro Verde"—green bird. His vivid coloring would lead one to believe him to be conspicuous in his habitat; but his furtiveness and the dominance of greens and yellows in his plumage keep him well hidden. True to their family traits, the Jays can be raucous, bullyish and overly-curious. Any human interruption of their common game of chasing each other through the trees will bring the group down from its haunts screaming and cawing at length. Nesting and rearing of young are conducted in heavily-wooded areas, after which they resume their roaming about, often living off the varied diets which may be found in towns or on ranches.

Like other Jays, male and female Green Jays look identical. They are similar in size to the Blue Jays, approximately eleven inches in length. The female in the porcelain composition has secured a wild persimmon, as the male prepares to do likewise. Typical of the Jay Family are the short, rounded wings, wide, rounded tail, and stout, sharply-pointed, all-purpose bills which can be used to hammer, split, tear or crush. The versatility of their bills accounts for their diversified diets. Of particular challenge to the artist was the "keying" of the brilliant blues, greens and yellows within the limitations set by the porcelain medium and available ceramic pigments.

Rufous Hummingbirds

(Selasphorus rufus)   PLATE 21

Hummingbirds, exclusively birds of the Americas, are charming and remarkable constituents of the bird world. The Rufous is among the most active of an active family and certainly is the champion traveler, ranging west of the Rockies from Alaska in summer to Mexico in winter. He portrays well the ethereal, evanescent characteristics common among all of his brethren. Diminutiveness of size, constant activity, dart-like, blurring swiftness, baffling aerodynamic artistry, and brilliancy of colors fanned by the sun's rays to produce one of nature's most exquisite kaleidoscopes. All should be privileged to witness the exciting courting acrobatics of the Rufous. He overwhelms his mate with a flight which carries him straight up into the air until only a flashing speck is visible against the sky; then a turn straight down brings him like a fiery meteor to pause fleetingly only an inch away from the female. Again and again he swings through his cycle with mesmerizing effect until he has won the heart of his lady.

As rendered in porcelain with Icelandic Poppies, the in-flight male is far more brilliant than his mate, with his dominant colors of cinnamon-rufous back, bronze-green head and metallic-scarlet chin and throat. The neck is long, the bill slender and awl-shaped, the feet small and underdeveloped, and the "hand" portion of the wing is much longer than the "arm" portion. The poppy bud and flower are removable from the sculpture for safety in transit and ease of handling.

Size of Sculpture: Height 14 inches; Width 9 inches.

A limited edition of 500 replicas.

Issued in 1966

PLATE 21

PLATE 22

Crested Flycatcher

PLATE 22

(Myiarchus crinitus)

Tyrant Flycatchers are exclusively American birds. The Crested is one of the more colorful of this mutely-colored family and ranges through the eastern United States and southern Canada. Among the common characteristics he shares with his family are extreme agility on the wing which enables him to catch flying insects with ease and grace, and a marked pugnacity toward crows, hawks and other large birds. Those which nest in the vicinity of poultry farms unknowingly serve as competent protectors. The singular characteristic which has made this bird famous is his curious habit of utilizing cast snake skins as the dominant material for his nest. Just why he does so has long been a matter of debate among ornithologists. Other names of the Crested are "Great Crested," "Great Crested Yellow-bellied," and "Snakeskin Bird."

In porcelain the male Crested Flycatcher is in an autumnal setting of sweet gum, one of our most beautiful fall trees. The gum leaves permanently are affixed with hand-fashioned metal stems. Distinctive physical features of the bird are long wings and tail, broad shoulders, short neck, large head, and a broad flattened bill gradually tapering to a sharp point, abruptly bent downward near the tip.

Size of Sculpture: Height 18½ inches; Width 14 inches.

A limited edition of 500 replicas.

Issued in 1967

Blue Grosbeak

The Blue Grosbeak, a member of the large Finch Family and close relative of the Cardinal, is located primarily in the southeastern Gulf and Atlantic states. His name "Grosbeak" was given because of his short, thick bill so useful for seed cracking and eating. Most feel that the Blue is not so handsome as his relatives, but this probably is due to the fact that he is a modest, timid bird. Even when he is seen in his wooded, shady haunts at close range his dark coloration usually leads to his identification as a Cowbird or other species. His song also is in keeping with his shy character—sweet but much weaker than those of his distinguished cousins. The Blue Grosbeak is called by one other name, "Blue Pop."

The setting and design of the sculpture portray the hesitating, suspicious nature of the Blue Grosbeak, hiding and peering from the protection of oak leaves and clusters. Although he is larger than many of his Finch relatives, he is similar to the family in most of his features—a heavy short bill, long and pointed wings, thick neck and head and broad feathers slightly rounded at the ends.

Size of Sculpture: Height 11 inches; Width 10 inches.

A limited edition of 750 replicas.

Issued in 1967

PLATE 23

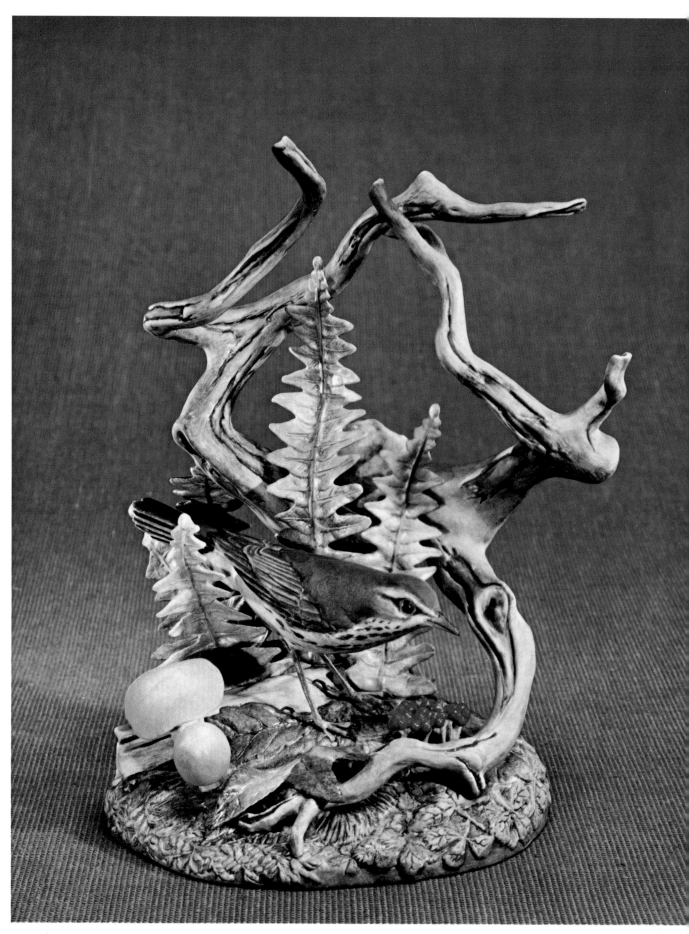

PLATE 24

The only features Water-Thrushes have in common with other Thrushes are coloration and a streaked breast. Manners are totally different and they are much smaller. In addition they are among the few birds which walk and bob in the mincing fashion of a Wagtail, tilting the body as they go, all the while oscillating the tail. Quick and nervous, they possess a song that trills with exuberance and sweetness. Activities and habitats usually are confined to the vicinity of wet grounds, streams and swamps. The Northern is the smallest of the Water-Thrushes and ranges through the northeastern states and eastern Canada. The confusion about color, habits and size is indicated by his many local names: "New York Warbler," "Small-billed Water-Thrush," "Wagtail," "Water Wagtail," "Aquatic Wood Wagtail," "Aquatic Thrush" and "New York Water-Thrush." An interesting feature of his nest is the building of a path-like doormat of leaves, sometimes a foot long, leading to the abode.

Elements of this bird's habitat form his porcelain environment—ferns, deadwood, mushrooms and cladonia lichen (commonly called "red-capped British Soldiers"). Male and female are identical in this and other Water-Thrushes. The Warbler-like characteristics are a slender and pointed short bill, indicative of insect eaters, long and pointed wings and a slightly notched tail.

Size of Sculpture: Height 10½ inches; Width 8½ inches.

A limited edition of 500 replicas.

Issued in 1967

Fledgling Canada Warbler

(Wilsonia canadensis)

PLATE 25

The Canada Warbler is a popular bird because of his sweet, liquid song and pleasing soft yellow breast with black tickings. He is a busy and relentless Warbler full of motion and energy as he darts in and out of the underbrush gleaning leaves and the air about for insects. His feeding actions are a combination of those of a Warbler and a Flycatcher. His territory is northcentral and northeastern North America touching only the northernmost tier of the United States. Nests are made in damp and dense coverts and usually near water, much like the Water-Thrushes. This beautiful little bird creates great excitement when seen by birdwatchers. His other names are "Canada Flycatcher," "Speckled Canada Warbler," "Necklaced Warbler" and "Canada Necklace."

The artist sculptured a fledgling Canada Warbler just out of the nest in a moment of his first frightening encounter. An exquisite Monarch Butterfly, as large as the fledgling, has paused above him. Both rest on a base and foliage representing a new feature. Three dimensional cutout work exposes the past season's leaves below the new spring growths. The Monarch presented a technical and artistic challenge. The legs are of gold which has been oxidized. The wings are so thin and translucent that extreme care need be taken in their firing and in matching the intricate color patterns and detail of opposite wing sides.

Size of Sculpture: Height 8½ inches; Width 8 inches.

A limited edition of 750 replicas.

Issued in 1967

PLATE 25

PLATE 26

Kestrels

PLATE 26

(Falco sparverius sparverius)

The Kestrel, a short-winged hawk with a low darting flight, is one of the numerous species of hawks used in the ancient sport of falconry, which dates back through history to 2000 B.C. in Central Asia. Today the Kestrel's relatives inhabit every country on earth. Known also as the "Rusty-Crowned Falcon" or "American Sparrow Hawk," this is the smallest and most sociable of American Hawks.

The artist depicted these birds perched on stumps, talons curved, eyes bright and alert. The female, which is similar to the male in size and coloration, is wearing the hood. The falconry regalia (all made of porcelain in the sculptures) is as originally conceived for their training in the courts of the Orient and used in pursuit of this ancient sport even today: jesses, 2 narrow strips of leather attached to each leg and to a short leash; bells, made at Lahore from a secret process and sought by falconers everywhere; and the hood, often gaily decorated, which serves as a blinder.

Size of Sculpture: Male Height 14 inches; Width 6 inches.

Female Height 16½ inches; Width 5½ inches.

A limited edition of 500 pairs.

Issued in 1968

Road Runner

The name "Road Runner" was given to this captivating bird because of his penchant for racing. He often has been seen attempting to out-distance a team of horses. Also known as the "Chaparral Cock," "Snake Killer," "Churca," "Paisano," "Lizard Bird" and "Correcamio," the Road Runner is considered one of the most striking creatures of the cactus belt of the Southwest. He is found in California, Colorado, Kansas, western and middle Texas, New Mexico, Arizona and the tableland of Mexico to Puebla. His nest is a large coarse structure of sticks, lined with grass, bark or snakeskin and hidden among the cacti or sagebrush. Lizards are the main sustenance of this bird, and even the young in the nest are fed on this reptile from the time they are out of the egg.

The Road Runner is approximately 20 inches in length. Male and female are identical in size and color. The feathers of the tail are long and graduated and the entire plumage is coarse and harsh. The artist depicted this bird in full pursuit of a horned toad.

PLATE 27

State Bird of: New Mexico
Size of Sculpture: Height 14 inches; Length 20½ inches.
A limited edition of 500 replicas.
Issued in 1968

PLATE 28

Size of Sculpture: Male Height 10½ inches; Width 11 inches.

                         Female Height 10½ inches; Width 6¾ inches.

A limited edition of 500 pairs.

Issued in 1968

Hooded Merganser

PLATE 28

(Lophodytes cucullatus)

The Hooded Merganser, a distinctively American bird, and the most beautiful of his family, is vivacious, elegant in form and graceful in movement. This lovely bird, also known as the "Hooded Sheldrake," "Water Pheasant" and "Fan-crested Duck" is found in North America at large and winters in southern British Columbia, across the United States about latitude 41° south to Lower California, Mexico, the Gulf States and Cuba. He is primarily a silent bird, but has a rather hoarse croak which is heard infrequently.

Exceedingly swift on the wing, the Merganser is a proficient diver and fast swimmer above and below surface and frequents clear streams and muddy pools alike. Although equipped with a toothed bill, he feeds on vegetable matter as well as on fish. The male bird has a thin, semi-circular crest which he can open and shut like a fan. The artist depicted the female Merganser preening her feathers while the male enjoys a chub.

Common Tern

The Common Tern, also named "Sea Swallow" or "Summer Gull," is found throughout the Northern Hemisphere, northern South America and Africa. He also breeds in Europe and Asia and winters in India and Africa.

Many naturalists assert that this webfooted species never dives and rarely swims, seeming to avoid the water except to procure food. When fishing, the Tern usually flies with bill pointing downward and, when observing his prey, dives like a flash to the surface, often immersing his head but seldom his entire body. The "Tee-arr, tee-arr" of the Terns as they gather for fishing, aids fishermen in locating schools of fish for their nets. Small fish, shrimp and small crustacea are the mainstay of the Tern's diet, augmented occasionally with grasshoppers and flying insects.

The Tern is approximately 16 inches in length. Both male and female are white, with a pale mantle of pearl-blue and a lustrous greenish-black crown extending to the lower level of the eyes. The sculpture shows the bird gracefully hovering over its eggs and newly hatched youngling among the rocks and pelagic remnants of a harsh, unvegetated terrain.

Size of Sculpture: Height 16 inches; Width 12 inches.

A limited edition of 500 replicas.

Issued in 1968

PLATE 29

PLATE 30

Young American Bald Eagle

PLATE 30

(Haliaeetus leucocephalus leucocephalus)

The young American Bald Eagle, named "Young America" by Mr. Boehm, specifically was designed for our incoming President in January 1969 as a symbol of vigor, determination and faith in our youth. As shown by the porcelain, the few-weeks-old eagle is immature in his plumage and charmingly awkward in his oversized physical characteristics. Even as a youngster, however, the eaglet possesses a proud, piercing, adventurous look—promise of the majestic adult he is to become three years hence.

During his maturing years the Bald Eagle also is called the "Black," "Gray" or "Washington Eagle," the latter a name given him by Audubon who thought he was a distinct species. His area extends throughout the rough, mountainous terrain of the United States south to northern Mexico, and he frequents the shores of lakes and rivers for food and drink. Mating is for life and year after year a pair will occupy the same nest—deserting their territory only occasionally when waters are frozen over and new food sources must be found.

The legendary eagle has inspired many literary tributes. Tennyson wrote of him:

> *He clasps the crags with crooked hands;*
> *Close to the sun in lonely lands,*
> *Ring'd with the azure world, he stands.*
> *The wrinkled sea beneath him crawls;*
> *He watches from his mountain walls,*
> *And like a thunder-bolt he falls.*

Size of Sculpture: Height 10 inches; Width 6 inches.

A limited edition of 850 replicas.

Issued in 1969

Western Bluebirds

The Western Bluebirds, sometimes called the California Bluebirds, are so similar in form, habits and disposition to the Eastern Bluebirds that only a trained eye can detect the color differences in the two species. His habitat ranges from the Pacific coast district to British Columbia, eastward through Oregon and Washington and in winter southward to lower California.

The Western Bluebird nests in the holes of dead trees between the trunk and loose bark, although in more populated areas he will nest in boxes supplied for that purpose. Like the Eastern he has a valued economic status. Large quantities of grasshoppers, caterpillars and beetles make up his diet, with an occasional side-dish of weedseeds and small fruit.

The male (deeper blue and with wings parted) and female Bluebirds are depicted in a single porcelain sculpture among six delicate clusters of wild yellow azaleas. The composition is extremely intricate structurally. The azalea flowers are comprised of well over 300 handcrafted, enameled, metal stems and stamens. The remaining components of the sculpture required the making of approximately 1200 mold sections.

PLATE 31

Size of Sculpture: Height 17 inches; Width 18 inches.

A limited edition of 400 replicas.

Issued in 1969

PLATE 32

PLATE 32 *(Auriparus flaviceps flaviceps)*

The Verdin, found in southwestern United States from southern California to Mexico, is an olive-gray bird about the size of his cousin the Chickadee. His distinctive yellow head also has caused him to be known as "Gold-Tit" or "Yellow-headed Bush-Tit."

For his home the Verdin has sparse pickings from which to build and small choice of area. His nest, tightly interwoven and lined with feathers, closely resembles a bundle of drift with a roof of thorns, and the doorway on the underside for protection. Although most birds abandon the nest as soon as their young have fledged, this bird, because of his tiny size, needs a protected place for sleep and so remains in the nest both summer and winter.

The Verdins of the sculpture are presented in a setting of Stewart Crucifixion-thorn, one of their favorite building materials. The male, high in the sculpture, has more yellow and chestnut on the head and epaulets. In the center of the composition is a bee whose detail is emphasized by its life-thin wings. An intricate pierced-work base reveals an underlayer of earth and older foliage.

Size of Sculpture: Height 9 inches; Width 9 inches.

A limited edition of 750 replicas.

Issued in 1969

Black-Headed Grosbeak

(Zamelodia melanocephala)   PLATE 33

The pure warbling song of the Black-Headed Grosbeak and his thin alarm note bears a remarkable resemblance to the sound of his eastern prototype, the Rose-Breasted Grosbeak. The male sings a pure and tender rhapsody while resting and working and even at high noon when other songsters fall silent. His looks match his song—handsome, flashy in flight, with a big beak—much in contrast to his attractive but subdued mate with her olive, buff and white coloring.

The Black-Headed is a native of Western United States and the plateau of Mexico, breeding south to southern portions of Mexico. In his habitat he also is called "Western Grosbeak" and "Black-Head." He prefers deciduous woods and shrubbery for nesting and living, although he will come freely around man's dwelling when assured of safety. On balance he is recognized as a friend of western orchardists. His diet includes early fruit, peas and beans but mainly consists of scale insects, canker worms, codling moths and flower beetles.

The male only is shown in the sculpture, his best finery partially cloaked by vine maple foliage. The airiness and freedom of the composition are aided by the incorporation with the porcelain of hand-fashioned metal stems supporting the hanging leaves and seed pods.

PLATE 33

Size of Sculpture: Height 10 inches; Width 13 inches.

A limited edition of 750 replicas.

Issued in 1969

PLATE 34

Size of Sculpture: Height 14 inches; Width 15 inches.
(with walnut base).

A limited edition of 500 replicas.

A biographical booklet about Adios accompanies each sculpture.

Issued in 1969

PLATE 34

Edward Marshall Boehm loved all forms of life. His early years as well as his later years as an artist were devoted to searching the beauty of nature, understanding it, perpetuating it through his work in animal husbandry and ornithology, presenting it with fidelity in his porcelain sculpture.

The great horse Adios was of special interest to Mr. Boehm. This sire epitomized the high standards of beauty, conformation and excellence sought by the artist; and, moreover, Adios was endowed with the genetic ability to pass on his attributes to his progeny. Adios sired hundreds of champion racers, studs and broodmares and dominated harness racing more completely than any other male in any sport.

Adios was born in 1940, died in 1965. He was by Hal Dale and out of Adioo Volo. He was the first horse to sire the winners of more than $1,000,000.00 in one year and he did it each year from 1956 through 1967. He sired 79 with records of 2:00 or faster for the mile distance. Through 1968 the get of Adios had won over $18,000,000.00. In 1968 his daughters produced the winners of close to $3,000,000.00. At public auction and in racing winnings his young constantly set new records. Among the great harness horses he sired are Bret Hanover, Adios Butler, Adios Harry and Bullet Hanover.

Adios' first years in stud were under the ownership and care of Mr. and Mrs. Delvin Miller at "Meadow Lands," near Washington, Pennsylvania. Later he was owned in a three-way syndicate by the Millers, Hanover Shoe Farms and Mr. Max Hempt. In October 1968, at his farm in Washington Crossing, New Jersey, Mr. Boehm presented the first porcelain sculpture of Adios to Mr. and Mrs. Miller.

Beau Brummells 1

PLATE 35

George Bryan Brummell lived from 1778 to 1840. Possibly no individual has had as much impact on proper dress and tidiness as Brummell. At the height of his popularity he was an intimate of George IV and wielded a dominating influence over the exclusive group of British society—a group known as the most brilliant in the history of England. His word was law on dress and manners. He was fashion's arbiter and a fierce apostle of bathing and grooming. Through his insistence an ideal of cleanliness was adopted both of the clothes and of the person—one of the many debts the modern world owes the early 19th-century dandy.

Mr. Boehm admired the elegance of Beau Brummell fashions. Through this elegance he felt he could best show his water-clear glaze and the beauty of good colors properly annealed. The porcelains point up the sartorial perfection of this rich period and the departure from earlier dress—a change from heavy satins, velvets and laces loosely fitted, to broadcloths and linens with excellent tailoring.

The primary principles of dress followed in the sculptures are Brummell's "good lines, good cloths, dark colors." To achieve richness and depth Mr. Boehm dipped into a dwindling cache of old Meissen colors he was fortunate in purchasing back in 1951. The browns, blacks and purples hold true in the kiln and compliment the beautiful glaze. The elegance of the figures is further enhanced by the coin gold of the base, buttons and fob and the solid gold hair pins of the lady.

PLATE 35

Size of Sculpture: Height 12 inches; Width 7 inches.

A limited edition of 500 pairs.

Issued in 1969

Edward Marshall Boehm Orchid Centerpiece

(Paphiopedilum Edward Marshall Boehm)   PLATE 36

In the fall of 1968 the Rod McLellan Company of South San Francisco, world leaders in the development and propagation of orchids, honored Mr. Boehm by naming a new hybrid after him. Furthermore, Mr. Boehm was asked to select a hybrid he personally liked, and he chose the subject of the sculpture, "Paphiopedilum Edward Marshall Boehm," a member of the Cypripedium family.

The first seed of Paphiopedilum E. M. B. was sown January 21, 1963 and it bloomed for the first time in early 1968.

The origin of the Paphiopedilum species is China and the Southeast Asian countries. They were introduced to Europe in the early 1800's and to the United States in the early 1900's. Following the second world war cross-hybridization with American hybrids largely occurred between English and American growers. This led to glorious new lines and the continuation here of naming new hybrids for famous people and royalty. Paphiopedilum remains, in the orchid family today, one of the most popular of cut flowers; and, it is one of the most easily grown orchids in the home and garden.

The hummingbirds of the sculpture are "Stellula calliope," two males and a female. This is the smallest and most elusive of North American Hummingbirds. They breed in the mountains of western North America, mainly west of the Sierras in the United States, from California to British Columbia, and winter chiefly in south-central Mexico. Stellula means "little star," calliope, "pleasant voiced." Other "gems" of the sculpture, a butterfly, "Neochera butleri," and two beetles, a female "Pharypia pulchella" and a male "Belionota sumptuosa."

PLATE 36

Size of Sculpture: Length 26 inches; Height 17 inches.

A limited edition of 300 replicas.

Issued in 1970

253

Oven-Bird

(Seiurus aurocapillus) PLATE 37

The confusion about the Oven-Bird, caused by its unusually varied gifts, is pointed up by its curious nicknames: "Golden-crowned Thrush", "Wood Wagtail", "Teacher", "Nightingale", and "Golden-crowned Accentor". It is Thrush-like in appearance, except for its striped head; like the Water-Thrush is one of the few walking terrestrial birds; incessantly bobs its tail in a jerky, comical manner; can rival the best songs of the Nightingale when moved to lyrical ecstasy; and, is so articulative in its song, reminds one of a teacher syllabicating for young students.

This ground-loving Warbler ranges North America, east of the Rocky Mountains. Those who have been fortunate to study its habits carefully have seen yet another of the Oven-Bird's distinctive peculiarities, the source of its real name. Akin to the structure of a Dutch oven, the female fashions an arched nest, partially imbedded in the ground, made of grass, leaves and plant fibers. It has a side entrance and is so skillfully blended with the forest floor cover, it is nearly impossible to find. No doubt many wandering, unfortunate ground insects, the main diet of the Oven-Bird, have unsuspectingly delivered themselves for dinner.

The bird of the sculpture represents both male and female, as sexes are identical. Its posture captures the perky, bobbing attitude of the Oven-Bird as it frolics amid its happy surroundings of Indian Pipe, ferns and Bracket fungus. The fern work is as delicate and as wispy as the hard-paste medium will allow. In its structure and terrestrial design, the composition harmonizes with that of the Boehm "Northern Water-Thrush" sculpture.

Size of Sculpture: Height 11 inches; Width 7 inches.
A limited edition of 750 replicas.
Issued in 1970

PLATE 37

Orchard Oriole

(Icterus spurius)   PLATE 38

When compared to its illustrious cousins, particularly the Baltimore Oriole, the Orchard Oriole is found to be much rarer with a more conservative plumage and a reserved countenance. It is so mild-mannered and polite it seems to win acceptance among even the most pugnacious species of birds. It makes its home in orchards throughout the Eastern United States and Mexico, inconspicuously busying itself with its chores and feeding from insects and fruit.

The most interesting trait is its errancy of instinct, its lack of subtlety, in affording maximum protection for its nestlings. Most wild creatures instinctively practice protective coloration in building their homes. The Orchard Oriole does just the opposite. Its nest, which is skillfully woven from fresh green grass and stalks, beautiful in proportion and color, is invisible among the leafy branches when first made. Later, at just about the time the helpless young are born, the grass has dried and the nest has turned yellow and brown making it clearly visible among its green surroundings!

The sculpture emphasizes the togetherness of these Orioles, perching on a beautiful tulip tree branch with blooms. Pairs usually work and cavort in concert. Whole families often are seen feeding together. The male has reached full plumage, a maturity requiring three years, and offers a pleasing contrast with its softly-colored mate. The tulip flower contains long porcelain stamens which, when hand-assembling in clay, require agility and a delicate touch. Each stamen is separately attached and supported so it will not bend and coalesce in the intense heat of the bisque firing.

PLATE 38

Size of Sculpture: Height 11 inches; Width 14 inches.

A limited edition of 750 replicas.

Issued in 1970

Beau Brummells II

PLATE 39

The first pair of Beau Brummel figures, in evening dress (see page 250), was introduced in 1969. The pair here illustrated features daytime wear.

PLATE 39

PLATE 39

Size of Sculptures: Height 11½ inches; Width 7 inches.
A limited edition of 500 pairs will be made.
Issued in 1970

Fondo Marino

PLATE 40

Only on rare occasions is an art piece created which is both a tour de force in its field as well as an object of uncommon beauty and excitement. Out of the studio of Edward Marshall Boehm, representing a culmination of twenty years of evolving skills and expressions, came that rare burst of creativity and energy that results in a masterpiece like the porcelain composition "Fondo Marino."

Fondo Marino, a busy portion of the sea in hard-paste porcelain, a coral reef in miniature, is as important a technical achievement as an artistic one. The sculpture demanded one and a half years of constant skilled craftsmanship in the making of the original model and its approximately 3400 mold sections. Individual molds involved in casting the separate model parts number 291. Dissection of the plasteline model into its components and accounting for those components through the mold making, casting and clay assembling stages, required an elaborate system of coding.

It is difficult to illustrate the intricacies of Fondo Marino. On the base the lace coral, in itself, has 39 separate cast sections. The Hermit Crab and its companion anemone, together, have 23 parts. Those familiar with prior Boehm sculptures may draw comparisons from the following: Fondo Marino has approximately 3½ times the mold and model parts of the "Western Bluebirds" and approximately six times those of the "Wood Thrushes."

Size is also critical in creating important pieces. For a description of the molding, casting and firing difficulties posed by another large sculpture, the "Ivory-billed Woodpeckers," refer back to pages 101 and 102. Parallel difficulties, of course, were experienced with Fondo Marino, particularly with the voluminous base and large coral parts. All of this before the subsequent challenges of assembling the many parts in clay, successfully propping and firing of the model in the bisque kiln, and the repeated hazards of the decorating kiln firings! The further along in the process, the greater the potential loss; and the probability of error is said to increase geometrically with increasing complexity. At any point in the long, hand-crafting process, an error in judgement or lack of concentration for a moment can result in the loss of the sculpture—an important

Size of Sculpture: Height 26 inches; Width 26 inches.

A limited edition of 50 replicas.

Issued in 1970

factor which must be allowed for in determining the economics of the piece and the number of models to be made in its edition.

The idea for an important marine sculpture originated from Mr. Boehm's love of the beauties of sea life. Through his twenty year career as an artist he maintained large collections of tropical fish and plant life in aquaria at his studio and gardens. He long had desired to do a marine sculpture, just one, and it would have to be the most intricate of this subject ever attempted. He waited several years for the right period—a time when the acceptance of his art was such to permit him and his artisans to expend the energy and resources necessary for a sculpture of the magnitude of Fondo Marino.

The teeming life of Fondo Marino includes sea anemones, sea horses, shells and starfish; several varieties of coral—staghorn, brain, mushroom and lace; and the following tropical fish: Rock Beauty (Holacanthus tricolor), Thorny-eyed Butterflyfish (Centropyge potteri), Longnose Butterflyfish (Forcipiger longirostris), and two varieties of Clownfish (Amphibrion percula and Amphibrion sebae).

PLATE 40

Fondo Marino

Hallmarks

The use of hallmarks was not carefully controlled in the early years of the studio. Although one can attempt to relate specific hallmarks to defined time periods, the results can only be considered approximations. We know that the hallmarks shown here are in correct chronological order; that "Osso Ceramics" was the first hallmark used by Mr. Boehm; and that the last two hallmarks were, in fact, adopted early in 1959 and remained the final marks used by Mr. Boehm. "Osso Ceramics" first was applied to pieces sometime early in 1950. The second, wreathed hallmark, bearing Mr. Boehm's name, probably was introduced late in 1951 and gradually replaced the original mark. This was followed by the horse's head which seems to have been designed late in 1952 and eventually replaced its predecessor. The decision to adopt the head was based on the fact that the very first of Mr. Boehm's sculptures accepted by a museum (The Metropolitan Museum of Art in 1951) was the "Percheron Stallion." "Boehm U.S.A." appears to have been introduced about 1954; but it might have been used in prior years for white, bisque subjects and during periods when the studio inadvertently ran out of decalcomanias or simply overlooked applying them. (The "U.S.A." also was necessary to separate Mr. Boehm's art from imports— and later was required when shipping to Canada was begun.) In summary, up to early 1959 hallmarks often were changed and overlapped in time. Since then the use of hallmarks has been precisely controlled.

OSSO CERAMICS
1950-1951

1951-1952

1952-1954

1959

Bibliography

CUSHION, JOHN P., *"Animals In Pottery And Porcelain,"* London:
Cory, Adams & Mackay Ltd., 1966.

GODDEN, GEOFFREY A. *"An Illustrated Encyclopedia of British Pottery And Porcelain,"* New York: Crown Publishers, Inc., 1966.

HARTMAN, URBAN, *"Pottery & Porcelain Marks,"* New York: Urban
Hartman, 1943.

LITCHFIELD, FREDERICK, *"Pottery And Porcelain,"* Fourth Edition,
New York: The Macmillan Company, 1925.

ORMSBEE, THOMAS H., *"English China And Its Marks,"* New York:
Deerfield Editions, Limited, 1959.

PICKMAN, DUDLEY LEAVITT, *"The Golden Age Of Porcelain,"* Boston: Dudley Leavitt Pickman, 1936.

SPARGO, JOHN, *"Early American Pottery & China,"* New York: The
Century Company, 1926.